# Hustles for Humanists

# Hustles for Humanists

## BUILD A BUSINESS WITH PURPOSE

Erica Machulak

Foreword by Crystal Marie Moten
Illustrated by Sophia van Hees

RUTGERS UNIVERSITY PRESS

New Brunswick, Camden, and Newark, New Jersey
London and Oxford

Rutgers University Press is a department of Rutgers, The State University of New Jersey, one of the leading public research universities in the nation. By publishing worldwide, it furthers the University's mission of dedication to excellence in teaching, scholarship, research, and clinical care.

978-1-97884082-9 (cloth)
978-1-9788-4081-2 (paper)
978-1-9788-4083-6 (epub)
978-1-9788-4084-3 (Web-PDF)

Cataloging-in-publication data is available from the Library of Congress.
LCCN 2024040397
A British Cataloging-in-Publication record for this book is available from the British Library.

Copyright © 2025 by Erica Machulak
All rights reserved
No part of this book may be reproduced or utilized in any form or by any means, electronic or mechanical, or by any information storage and retrieval system, without written permission from the publisher. Please contact Rutgers University Press, 106 Somerset Street, New Brunswick, NJ 08901. The only exception to this prohibition is "fair use" as defined by U.S. copyright law.

References to internet websites (URLs) were accurate at the time of writing. Neither the author nor Rutgers University Press is responsible for URLs that may have expired or changed since the manuscript was prepared.

∞ The paper used in this publication meets the requirements of the American National Standard for Information Sciences—Permanence of Paper for Printed Library Materials, ANSI Z39.48-1992.

rutgersuniversitypress.org

*For Omar, who knew the risks*
*and jumped with me anyway*

# Contents

*Foreword by Crystal Marie Moten*    ix

*Prologue*    xiii

1. Choose Your Own Adventure    1

How to Use This Book    21

2. Translate Your Strengths into Services    37

3. Name Your Price    67

4. Connect with Your Clients    93

5. The Low-Key Launch Plan    121

6. Grow Your Own Way    143

*Acknowledgments*    155

*Notes*    157

*Image Credits*    163

*Index*    165

# Foreword

Growing up on the south side of Chicago in the 1980s and 1990s, to a working-class, single Black mother, I knew a few things for sure. I loved Black history, literature, and culture. I was going to be a teacher. *And, I wasn't going to be poor.* I had seen and experienced firsthand the struggle of trying to make ends meet, living paycheck to paycheck, and depending on food stamps to fill the refrigerator once a month. While my family and household were rich in spirit, encouragement, and culture, our pocketbooks were meager. And this was okay; we lived, I thrived. I went to college on a scholarship, went to graduate school on a fellowship, and got my first full-time job as a college history professor. From the outside, I was Black Excellence *and* #BlackGirlMagic personified. I made it.

Except—what does "making it" mean? In my world, heavily influenced as it was by growing up in a Black Christian family and being surrounded by Black women doers who often sacrificed their personal well-being for community uplift, making it meant going to school, getting a good job, and being active in your community. "Making it" for me also meant fulfilling my purpose and passion of sharing Black history with the broadest audiences possible. I thought, somewhere, along the way, that my passion would manifest into money.

And it did. It has. And I feel guilty, sometimes.

Why? Because I received the subliminal message that no one got rich off (or should get rich off) being a history teacher. And, in fact, financial struggle was/is a crucial part of the job description. It's not a secret that teachers are some of the most poorly paid professionals in the United States. But, while it is true that becoming a history teacher won't make a person rich, it shouldn't cause one to live beneath the poverty line, either. And to be clear, I am not rich, not even close!

Looking back on my professional story, I wish *Hustles for Humanists* was around when I was trying to figure out not only how to "make it"

x  Foreword

but also what "making it" meant for me. Teacher. Lawyer. Doctor. Postal worker. Nurse. Secretary. Those were the careers I knew about. My interests most aligned with being a teacher. However, as a person passionate about and deeply invested in using my skills and power to make a difference in the world, and specifically for people of African descent and also as a person with the life experience of wondering whether I'd have access to the basic resources to maintain life—food, shelter, health care—this book would have helped me think more expansively, *and differently*, about using my skills for the betterment of myself and humanity, through entrepreneurship or other means.

In 1979, the Black feminist, lesbian, mother, warrior poet Audre Lorde penned what, arguably, could be one of the most quoted sentences in Black feminist writing: "for the master's tools will never dismantle the master's house" ("Master's Tools," in *Sister Outsider*, 1979, 112). Many activists from various backgrounds who consider themselves outside of the system or on the margins have used the sentiment behind this powerful statement to forge new ways to transform their worlds. The quote is extremely meaningful, but like most quotes plucked from a longer context, there's more to it. Lorde wrote these words in a piece in which she was reflecting on her participation in a humanities conference where she had been called upon to discuss "the role of difference within the lives of American women: difference of race, sexuality, class, and age" (110). While at this conference, Lorde realized that her panel was the only one that included Black feminists and lesbians. Centering the perspectives of "those of us who stand outside of this society's circle of acceptable women," Lorde asserted what those "who have been forged in the crucible of difference" have been intimately aware of: how to survive (112). Survival is transforming differences into strengths and understanding the master's tools, which Lorde noted, "may allow us to temporarily beat him at his own game, but . . . will never allow us to bring about genuine change." Lorde understood that those who benefit from unjust structures would feel threatened by this, especially those "who still define the master's house as their only source of support" (112).

Sometimes it feels as if we humanists have conceded two things: (1) money as a tool of the master and (2) the master's house as our sole source of support.

Considering Audre Lorde's famous quote made me wonder, What are the master's tools? For too long, I think some humanists have considered money to be a tool of the master, and this has been to our detriment. Some are influenced by their faith traditions that assert that "money is evil" (when really it is the love of money, or greed, that is questionable). Others are critical of how capitalism stratifies those who have money and those who don't. The truth of the matter is that money makes the world go around, and it can either go around and be used by those with humanity's best interest at heart or be used to oppress. In the world we live in today, it can't *not* be used.

The second point feels more difficult because it can be frightening to disinvest oneself from whatever structure of support one has traditionally relied on. However, *Hustles for Humanists* provides one way forward. Disinvesting from the master's house and investing in oneself and one's community directly might feel like going it alone, but that is not what Erica Machulak suggests when she offers entrepreneurship as a potential way forward for humanists. Machulak offers insight into why entrepreneurship could be a productive way forward, breaks myths related to building a purposeful business, and provides practical guides to get started on one's journey.

In recent years, it seems like the humanities have been playing a losing game. Humanists consistently lament attacks on certain humanistic lines of inquiry, decreasing professional opportunities and higher workloads, and a general disinvestment writ large. Instead of framing our work through this loss, *Hustles for Humanists* acknowledges what we are up against and offers a meditation, and actionable steps, on what humanists have to gain when we pour our energy and skills into creating new, more sustainable and ethical ways of doing, and funding, our work.

Crystal Marie Moten
*public historian, curator, and writer*

# Prologue

There's a moment in the *Canterbury Tales* that has been stuck in my brain for the past decade. Chaucer's famous pilgrims run into the Canon's Yeoman, an apprentice to an alchemist who, he claims, "can pave all the streets in silver and gold." The Yeoman vacillates between admiration and slander for the Canon, talking the company's ear off about his many wonders while also signaling that his boss isn't totally on the up and up. We can practically hear the Host wanting to throttle the Canon's neck as he exclaims, exasperated, "But is he a clerk, or noon?" In modern terms, the Host is asking whether or not the Canon is a scholar.

This question of what makes one a scholar haunted my dissertation. I spent two weeks in the University of Notre Dame's paleography room trying to understand the St. Scholastica Riots, sparked by a fourteenth-century bar brawl between Oxford students and townspeople. I fell in love with medieval dream theory, the great loophole of literary tradition that enabled nontheologians to experiment with fiction, deferring to the experts to determine whether their dreams were credible. I became more broadly obsessed with prologues by authors and translators who found the maneuvers to justify, through a careful balance of self-deprecation and strategic citations, the audacious act of writing in vernacular languages like French and English.

My research unfolded in tandem with my search inward to decide for myself what it means to be a scholar. About halfway through my PhD program, three life events rewired my brain to think differently about my future. First, I bombed my comprehensive exams. Okay, fine, I was asked to retake *parts* of my comprehensive exams after the summer. This was the first time that I had experienced what felt like true failure. It made me question whether I deserved to be a scholar, and it gave me my first taste of academic politics. Second, I met my now-husband at the Middlebury Language Schools' immersion program. After eight weeks of flirting in broken Arabic, he went back to Boston, and I returned to Indiana. The ensuing years of long distance impressed on me how much geography mattered to me. Third, my parents called to tell me that my mom had Stage 4 brain cancer. I dropped what I was doing and drove four hours to her hospital room in Milwaukee.

In retrospect, it was telling that I got my first scholarly article accepted, pending revisions, on the same day that I learned about her diagnosis. Over the next year, I loosened my grip on teaching, publications, and any other professional activities that weren't critical to getting my degree. By default, I stopped doing the things that would make me competitive on the academic market. When my mom died, it occurred to me that I had no desire to pursue the tenure track. I learned a few weeks before her passing that my best friend, a fellow medievalist, and I had been awarded fellowships to teach in London. While there, we co-organized field trips to take our students to castles, plays, crypts, and archives all over the city.

After that, my career plan started to come together. I got an internship at the National Endowment for the Humanities, where phenomenal mentors taught me how to write for public audiences. I came back from the internship with a new fellowship to finish my dissertation and no desire to try for the academic market. I targeted my job search on cultural institutions and other nonprofits in Washington, DC. Right when I got an offer for an entry-level job with my dream employer, the Smithsonian, my partner landed a tenure-track position in Vancouver, Canada. Surprise! I was back to snakes and ladders, this time with designated support for spousal hires and a much better idea of how to position my experience for potential employers.

I would not have described any of these early career steps as "goal oriented." At the time, they felt like more of the same intuitive leaps and lucky strikes that had led me to graduate school in the first place. What I have since come to realize, however, is that I was slowly zeroing in on what are now very clear priorities for my personal and professional life: public scholarship, creative control over my work, and the flexibility to spend a lot of time with my geographically dispersed family. It took me a little bit longer to figure out what that best life costs and how to make it possible.

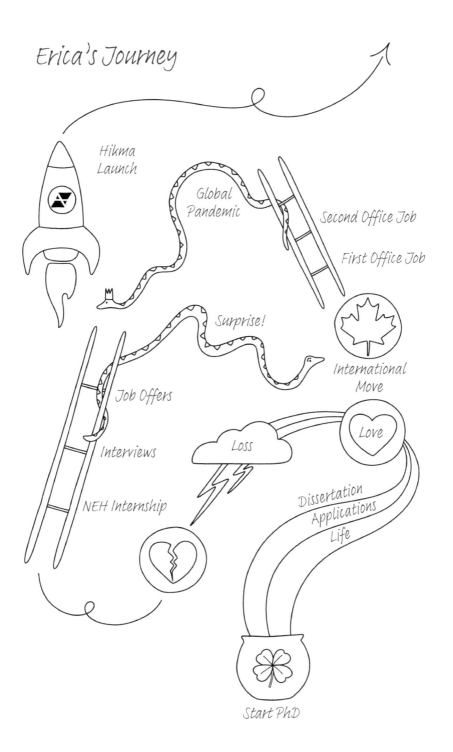

xvi Prologue

Clarifying my priorities and setting new goals enabled my partner and me to make the informed decision driving this book: I quit my job and launched my business.

Since launching Hikma in October 2020, I've been delighted to rediscover the things I loved most about being a scholar as they manifest in new forms. I get to chase questions I care about, build relationships with amazing colleagues, design and teach courses of my choosing, and create my own methodologies to address knowledge and market gaps. Even better, I get to work with public scholars across disciplines who are developing trauma-informed testimony collection practices, using robots to make buildings more sustainable, creating portable ultrasounds for and with rural and Indigenous communities, and driving all sorts of positive change in other spaces. Somehow, I have figured out how to make a comfortable living while collaborating with brilliant, kind people on initiatives that align with my values. The road is not easy, but it is possible.

This is the book that I wish I could have read in my final years of graduate school, when I was struggling to imagine what my next steps could look like beyond the academy. It's the book that I wish I could have reread a year or so after graduation, when I had published a couple of freelance articles with the National Endowment for the Humanities and built more confidence in my professional voice. Finally, it's the book I could have read at the start of the pandemic, when, after holding several staff roles in higher ed, I decided to quit my job and launch my business. At each stage, I needed not only practical advice but also a framework to help me build my own process and chart my own path.

I've written this book with graduate students and emerging scholars in mind to respond to the erosion of the tenure-track job market and the precarious position in which thousands of emerging humanities PhDs now find themselves as a result. It is inspired by questions from hundreds of early-career scholars and practitioners that I've fielded over Zoom coffees and during training programs since launching my business. It is a love letter to the humanities and, especially, to my countless friends and colleagues who were (and, in some cases, still are) editing theses, transcribing documents, indexing monographs, and taking on countless other side hustles for far less pay than they deserve.

Part framework, part phrase book, and part field guide, *Hustles for Humanists* draws together language and learnings from entrepreneurship, design thinking, knowledge mobilization, and public scholarship. It is designed to help you think more expansively about your options and design your next steps on your terms. My hope is that the tools and strategies provided will help you make your own discoveries with intention and confidence.

# Hustles for Humanists

# 1

# Choose Your Own Adventure

## 2 HUSTLES FOR HUMANISTS

# This Is How We Save the World

Launching a start-up in the first year of the pandemic was, for me, an experience of chaotic, continuous learning. As I filed the papers to claim my business name, I imagined myself curled up in my reading nook, sipping tea and leafing through a curated list of books and articles about entrepreneurship, industry trends, and personal growth. When I met with my first potential client on my first day open for business, it became immediately clear that the market had other ideas. All of my curiosities about entrepreneurship came together in one urgent question: What could I offer to the person right in front of me in exchange for real money?

The answer to this question sparked a cascade of new ones. How much should I charge? What should the contract say? Where, when, and how would the project unfold? How would I collect payments? Every one of these questions created new threads that were deeply satisfying to unravel. Even as I listen to my bank's hold music and squint my eyes at tax collection regulations, the monotony and anxiety are made more bearable by the enjoyment I take from figuring things out that serve a purpose and move my work forward. Being a business owner continues to fill me with agency, curiosity, and joy.

In addition to the many challenges that come with starting any business, this cultural moment was particularly complicated. When I launched Hikma in October 2020, the world was still trying to figure out how to keep spinning during a pandemic that would clearly last a lot longer than many of us had anticipated. Employees took flight en masse in the Great Resignation. Universities scrambled to build virtual classrooms, and graduate students and administrators alike watched the tenure track evaporate even faster than it was doing before the pandemic. The Black Lives Matter movement and biblical-level climate catastrophes demanded that funders, businesses, universities, and individuals take a hard look at their social and climate responsibilities.

As I started my business, I faced constant reminders that the world was literally and figuratively burning down around us—and that we need change in deep, complex ways. The polarization of our civic dialogues and difficulty of connecting decision-makers with reliable information added fuel to the fire. A cursory look at the United Nations Sustainable Development Goals shows how much work we have to do and the many pathways needed to save our planet and the people in it. While there are any number of technologies that might solve targeted problems, inventions alone will not save the world. Physical and digital products must be complemented with people who can interpret context, anticipate the implications of new ideas, and monitor the implementation of new tools for unanticipated consequences on our world. The systems-level change we so desperately need requires people who lead with empathy and thrive in ambiguity. The world needs humanists.

We are in an unprecedented moment of creativity to reimagine what the humanities are and can be. More than that, we are in an unprecedented moment to reimagine the role that humanists play so that we can make meaningful and responsive contributions to a complicated world. I have never heard this expressed more succinctly than by Lonnie Bunch, the Smithsonian secretary and founding director of the National Museum of African American History and Culture. In dialogue with Johnetta Cole at the 2020 National Humanities Conference, Bunch said, "One of the greatest strengths of the humanities is not even the content that we give but helping the public embrace ambiguity."[1] Humanists' comfort with ambiguity, it turns out, is also an asset in the business world. In a survey led by the Harvard Business School professor Linda A. Hill, fifteen hundred executives identified the following as "the leadership traits most critical to success in digital transformation": adaptability (71 percent), curiosity (48 percent), creativity (47 percent), and comfort with ambiguity (43 percent).[2] Frameworks like the United Nations Sustainable Development Goals and B Corporation Certification have provided new shared language for organizations across industry and the social sector to find points of alignment, which is the first step to identifying creative solutions to some of the world's most complicated challenges.[3]

We rise to these challenges by recognizing what we have to offer and bringing those attributes to new situations. That transformation is an act of translation that requires us to recognize strengths in others and consider how the things we bring may complement and amplify assets that already exist in other contexts. Humanities scholars trade in complexity

4 HUSTLES FOR HUMANISTS

and storytelling. We are writers, editors, translators, analysts, and unknotters of problems that defy easy answers. When we write our dissertations, we manage long-term, evolving projects that require negotiation with leadership. When we teach, we facilitate dialogues, develop rubrics, and build group consensus. In the knowledge economy, these deeply honed "soft skills" are aces in our pockets. Whether you are looking for inspiration, reinforcing your freelance work, or ready to launch a full-time business, I hope that the chapters that follow will help you recognize your value and position yourself to approach any professional pathway from a place of strength.

This book is a field guide for humanists who want to find or create meaningful work. That might mean transforming your ad hoc freelance work into an intentional side hustle, building out your side hustle into your sole source of income, or simply reframing the value of your labor so that you can think more expansively about your options. For our purposes, "humanists" are people who have the relentless curiosity to steep themselves in ambiguous questions for years on end. They are also concerned with the ethical implications of the answers they discover along the way. There are brilliant, deeply rigorous humanists working across our knowledge ecosystem as curators, lawyers, policy makers, publishers, not-for-profit directors, start-up founders, and in other roles, many of whom have inspired the chapters that follow. Not all humanists have PhDs, and a PhD is not required to advance complex, purpose-driven work that helps build a more just and caring world.

Growing a business has built my confidence in my own ability to figure things out and make contributions in the contexts that matter most to me. It has also lit a pathway to a life of creativity, joy, and self-determination. Every dimension of my business has benefited from the following principles:

- Know your worth
- Appreciate strengths in others
- Nurture relationships
- Craft your own story

You cannot advance these principles without a focus on relationships and process. Whether you want to make your business your sole source of income or use it as a stepping-stone to other professional opportunities, these principles will enrich both your process and your outcomes.

# Why the World Needs Humanists

Before we dive in, one caveat to our focus on purpose-driven work: "saving the world" doesn't have to mean making social justice, climate justice, or any other do-gooder cause the focus of your business. The beauty of entrepreneurship is that you get to choose what your purpose is and how you want to realize it. That might mean founding an animal shelter or building a nonprofit that supports underserved youth through urban gardening, but it could also mean having coffee with a potential mentee who wants to learn how you built your book-editing side hustle. Job creation, transparent marketing, good governance, and relationship building are just some of the ways that business owners within and beyond the humanities can level up the practice of entrepreneurship, redefine the future of work, and create pathways for aspiring entrepreneurs from underserved communities to access the hidden curricula of our capitalist reality.

The skewed distribution of venture capital funding in the United States is indicative of equity gaps in entrepreneurship. McKinsey reports that only 1 percent of VC funding went to Black founders and 1.5 percent to Latino founders in 2022.[4] An article published by the Center for Strategic and International Studies indicates that "limited social networks," "fewer role models," and "skew in fields of education" are some of the key roadblocks to explain why women receive less than 3 percent of all VC funding.[5] By figuring out how to access bigger pieces of the pie, humanists can build new networks, create new leadership positions, and decode the jargon and protocols of business culture. By sharing these learnings and opening up our communities to underrepresented talent, we can foster more diverse, equitable, and inclusive landscapes of practice. No matter the shape, size, or wares of your business, you can apply your humanities

**6** HUSTLES FOR HUMANISTS

lens to make our world better. This book is designed to help you think more expansively about your options and design your next steps on your terms.

# The Myths We Tell Ourselves

There are myths that others tell us—and that we tell ourselves—that hold humanists back from pursuing work that fills both our hearts and our bank accounts. When I first started talking to my humanities colleagues about starting my business, I encountered a lot of skepticism. Some pushed back that I was wasting my potential as a medievalist, casting away three prestigious degrees, a promising dissertation, and a world of "intellectual freedom" to write other people's grants. The message, as I took it, was that I was a sellout trading in my life of the mind for a few tawdry baubles. These conversations were familiar to me from my final year of graduate school, when I had made known that the mysteries of "alt ac" were calling and that I would not be taking up the tenure-track circuit. I consider myself lucky that the tenure track had lost its appeal around the time of my comprehensive exams. By the time I launched Hikma, I was already quite confident that entrepreneurship would bring its own intellectual challenges, and my curiosity was piqued.

The second stream of pushback that I received when I started my business is one that I continue to grapple with as a consultant who works primarily with clients in higher ed. I encountered many humanists who saw the value (or economic imperative) of freelancing as a scholar but who made all sorts of calculus to determine what was or wasn't ethical when starting an enterprise at the heart of a capitalist system. Words like "neoliberal" were used liberally. The concept of "competition" was tut-tutted. Calling my business a "hustle" and saying out loud that I *enjoyed* the hustle? Well, that was just crass. To me, the general sentiment seemed to be that one could start a business out of economic necessity and a rejection of the systemic problems with other organizations, provided that one didn't enjoy making money or consort with those who do.

## *Myth 1. The Academy Is the Only Place Where You Can Be a Scholar*

"What does being a scholar mean to you?" Hikma's research partners at the University of British Columbia, Andrea Webb and Jillianne Code, asked this question to fifty-five PhDs across Canada, the US, and the UK through a 2022 survey. All but one of the participants wrote responses in the open text field, some of them as long as two to three paragraphs. The takeaway? Scholarship has far more to do with agency, curiosity, and self-determination than with your institutional affiliation.[6]

Just because your academic mentors may not have the lived experience to communicate your options doesn't mean that you don't have options. As Loleen Berdahl and Jonathan Malloy write in *Work Your Career*, "PhD programs are taught at universities by people who previously earned PhDs and now have tenure-track jobs, and these programs revolve around the study of scholarly peer-reviewed research written by other people at universities with PhDs and tenure."[7] In *"So What Are You Going to Do with That?,"* Susan Elizabeth Basalla and Maggie Debelius synthesize a common pattern that they have identified in their many interviews with "postacademic" professionals: "Instead of making a U-turn in the middle of their lives, most of these alumni followed up on a lifelong interest or a half-forgotten talent by traveling a parallel path toward an equally fulfilling destination."[8] To think that scholars only work in universities is a failure of imagination.

The tenure track is far from the only pathway to sustainable employment and a purpose-driven life. For many humanists, finding joy in labor is closely tied to opportunities to learn, create knowledge, and contribute to sustained, generative conversations. Among academics, there is a prevalent misconception that these elements can only be had in traditional scholarly pathways. There is also significant professional pressure to give up a living wage, geographic mobility, and professional agency to keep one's hat in the tenure-track ring. As a result of this pressure, many emerging scholars make astonishing sacrifices to keep themselves in the running. And yet, there's no guarantee that this pathway will even bring the kind of intellectual fulfillment that so many imagine it will. Entrepreneurship

**8** HUSTLES FOR HUMANISTS

is a pathway to do the things about being a humanist that you love doing without having to sacrifice happiness, economic stability, or purpose.

If the idea of striking out on your own makes you feel lonely, know that there is a community of smart, creative entrepreneurs who have been where you are and are waiting to welcome you. The term "independent scholar" so often applied to people doing academic research without academic resources conjures an image of an underemployed PhD operating mostly alone, occasionally making an appearance at a relevant academic conference. Every independent scholar I know has leveraged their research to lead differently, build community, and make meaningful contributions to their field. Instead of being an independent scholar, imagine yourself as a *community* scholar with the agency to explore ideas without disciplinary constraints, create and publish through the channels that make sense to you, and build the professional relationships that will enable you to thrive.

This paradigm shift can be freeing—and it is a better reflection of how many scholars work outside of formal institutional employment. The community scholar engages in vibrant conversations about new ideas irrespective of discipline or communication channel. Community scholars recognize the benefits of truly cross-field knowledge exchange and the power of collaboration. They are curious, and they treat knowledge gaps as opportunities to build relationships and contribute to wider, richer conversations. Professionals with rigorous humanities training are well equipped to carry their scholarly selves into their field of choice, whether that's within the academy, in government, in the social sector, in industry, or through organizations of their own design. By harnessing the principles of entrepreneurship, they can build the strategies, competencies, and resilience to create space for curiosity and joy in any context.

Community scholars across professional contexts are creating spaces and dialogues to reexamine whether and how the humanities serve (and, by extension, humanists serve) society. This conversation has become a crossroads for multimodal dialogue that intertwines peer-reviewed publications with scholarly society programs, philanthropic priorities, journalism, and social media. Much of this conversation is driven by academics with extensive hands-on experience in higher ed administration.

In *Putting the Humanities PhD to Work*, Katina Rogers writes, "As measures of success become more expansive, the conservative nature of the university is loosened, and the institution slowly moves away from valorizing a particular kind of knowledge that is also bound up with whiteness and elitism."[9] Rogers, founder of Inkcap Consulting, is one of many humanities PhD alums finding creative pathways for change through for-profit mechanisms.

Perhaps the most damaging myth of all is that humanists lack the "marketable skills" to offer meaningful contributions beyond the academy. Even when we manage to shed these assumptions on an individual level, the fear that our academic colleagues will judge us for striking out—or that our prospective clients will find our skills lacking—is enough to keep smart, talented, highly trained professionals in a perpetual state of underemployment and unpaid labor for years, if not decades.

**KEY TAKEAWAY**

You get to decide whether and how you want to be a scholar.

## Myth 2. I Don't Know the First Thing about Running a Business

When I launched Hikma, I was pleasantly surprised to discover that I already had a side hustle. I had been writing—and getting paid for—articles for the National Endowment for the Humanities for several years, building on relationships and skills I had developed as an intern midway through my PhD. While I hadn't freelanced regularly enough to pay the rent, I had learned how to pitch an article, send an invoice, and talk to my editor about a tricky draft. As I negotiated writing projects with new clients, I could feel those neurons firing again. So many of my academic colleagues build connections and supplement their incomes with short-term

## 10 HUSTLES FOR HUMANISTS

projects like indexing, translating, and editing on the side. If this is you, make no mistake: you are a business owner.[10]

In *Where Research Begins*, Thomas S. Mullaney and Christopher Rea describe "research" as "a process not just of solving problems but of finding problems that you—and other people—didn't know existed. It's a process of discovery, analysis, and creation that can generate its own momentum and create a virtuous circle of inspiration."[11] These same competencies are critical to building a business. Humanists are specifically trained for "discovery, analysis, and creation" that consider context, surface patterns, and drive pathways of inquiry, where the act of asking a question involves knowing that the transformation often takes place within the question itself. Critiquing and transforming the questions we ask as our context shifts is the thing that sets us apart, and that flexibility and comfort with ambiguity is what enables us to make progress in an environment that is anything but controlled. As Robert Weisbuch asks in *The Reimagined PhD*, "Why should we settle for *critiquing* when we might play a far greater role in *constructing* the public world?"[12] Where Weisbuch creates a binary between "critiquing" and "constructing," entrepreneurship offers a way to do both.

Founders get impostor syndrome, too, and for similar reasons. It comes with the territory of carving out a path forward while constantly trying to learn in an environment of ambiguity. I first noticed this trend during an entrepreneurship panel at the 2020 American Historical Association Conference. On that panel, Michael Tworek, PhD in history and founder of the start-up Polis, asserted that humanists are natural entrepreneurs because we are "autodidacts"; that is, we are good at figuring things out by asking the right questions and identifying the resources to answer them. This work of self-teaching is also essential to entrepreneurship, but the jargon of the start-up world can obscure lessons that are, when you get down to it, intuitive for and already practiced by many humanists.

What is stopping humanists from becoming entrepreneurs? The greatest obstacle to this transformation is one of language, not values. The vocabulary of entrepreneurship is crowded by the language of competition and disruption, privileging technology over ethics and speed over nuance. Entrepreneurship is an act of translation and self-teaching. Your curiosity, empathy, and ability to teach yourself are strengths that are too often underrated. You already have the skills and capacity to do this. Learning the language, frameworks, and tools will help you do it more intentionally and efficiently. Once you gain basic fluency in business speak, it becomes much easier to shift your mindset about your value. Trust me: you already know how to do this.

**KEY TAKEAWAY**

You know more than you think you do, and you can learn the rest.

## Myth 3. Money Is Dirty

Real talk: staying broke will not help you create the change you want to see in the world. If you are reading this book, it's unlikely that you are at risk of becoming the world's next ethically questionable tech billionaire. Some humanists are uncomfortable thinking and talking about money, let alone assigning a dollar amount to their work. Some don't have the luxury of worrying about it. Very little of our humanities training prepares us to think about our labor in terms of monetary value. Indeed, our understanding of our worth is undercut by the norms of compensation within higher ed, where we receive stipends instead of salaries, honoraria instead of facilitation fees, and where, far too often, prestige is treated as a viable replacement for adequate health care. The presumed nobility of the scholarly profession has reinforced a disconnection between labor and compensation that is baffling to most people outside the academy.

There are legitimate reasons to be skeptical about entrepreneurship, particularly when we consider the dubious role that many start-ups and larger corporations play today in our political systems, our access to information, and our carbon footprints. The reality is that, in our current

## 12  HUSTLES FOR HUMANISTS

moment, it is not possible to insulate ourselves from capitalism. It is possible to interrogate the mechanisms of capitalism, analyze the problems we are most driven to solve, and implement models that address those problems. An increasingly diverse community of social entrepreneurs is actively organizing, holding each other accountable, and building better practices that prioritize not profit for profit's sake but revenue as a means to treat employees well, promote equitable access, and implement practices that support human health and the environment.

What better way to challenge the system than to build something better from the inside? Money is a tool to do so. As Crystal Marie Moten points out in the foreword, "The truth of the matter is that money makes the world go around, and it can either go around and be used by those with humanity's best interest at heart or be used to oppress. In the world we live in today, it can't not be used." Money enables us to support ourselves, create employment opportunities, and build processes that are ethical and sustainable. As Joel Solomon and Tyee Bridge write in *Clean Money Revolution*, "We can find joy and meaning beyond unlimited consumption. The wealth that has perpetuated injustice can transform our world."[13] Humanists are more than capable of designing businesses that thrive, as we do, in environments of profound ambiguity. As many caregivers learn the hard way, we are better prepared to serve others when we first make sure that we ourselves are healthy, secure, and able to thrive. As Madeleine Shaw puts it in *The Greater Good*, "Working yourself into a state of ill health or bankrupting your business is not going to serve anyone."[14] It is in our collective best interest to build and share better models than the ones currently available to us.

It's important to note that not everyone has the luxury of worrying about whether they should get paid for their work. When we accept financial precarity in the name of meaningful work, we devalue our labor and the labor of our colleagues. In this way, do-gooders with the means to undercharge can reinforce barriers to people who suffer most from systemic inequities. Humanists have a massive opportunity to build better practices within industry that can serve as models for businesses seeking to do better. To build and sustain those practices for the long term, though, we must find ways to build services, partnerships, and business models that can thrive within the markets as they exist today.

## KEY TAKEAWAY

Money is a tool that you can use to pay your rent, create opportunities, and fix broken systems.

# On Playing with Fire

Humanists have a long history of using storytelling to interrogate our systems. Well before modern conversations about carbon footprints, the Environmental, Social & Governance (ESG) Framework, and the UN Sustainable Development Goals, ancient Greek philosophers spotted the danger of innovation without forethought. Any time I hear a start-up founder glorifying "disruption" for disruption's sake, I think of Prometheus stealing fire for humanity. In Greek mythology, Prometheus appears as both a trickster and humanity's savior, giving people the tools to survive without considering how his intervention will play out. Plato's *Protagoras* uses the Prometheus myth to complicate the legal system and interrogate assumptions about good governance.

As Plato tells it, Prometheus's theft is a quick fix to cover up a careless mistake and balance out the ecosystem. Prometheus and his brother, Epimetheus, are assigned the task of ensuring sustainability across the animal kingdom by endowing each species with traits to balance out the others. During the final check, Prometheus realizes that his brother has left humanity out. He pilfers Hephaestus's fire and Athena's mechanical arts, thinking that these tools will correct the mistake and restore equilibrium among the world's species. The plan backfires, of course, as people

## 14 HUSTLES FOR HUMANISTS

quickly slide from cooking and lighting altars to destroying each other with "dispersion and destruction." Only when Zeus introduces the "art of government" do things get back on track.[15]

We see echoes of this narrative in today's start-up world, where new technologies are emerging too quickly for policies around them to be fully considered and applied. Social media corporations are designing the dominant tools of our world on the basis of data that privileges the needs of their most lucrative customers. Fast fashion is endangering thousands of workers around the world to sell us five-dollar novelty T-shirts. The rapid colonialism of outer space is generating tons of garbage without global policies for waste management. Profit-driven organizations can and do damage climates, communities, and human health when the pursuit of profit outweighs the implementation of ethical and sustainable practices. Consumers and organizations alike make daily decisions about which trade-offs serve our values best within the parameters of the moment. As new technologies and globalization present new inequities all around us at warp speed, dragging our feet is dangerous.

We will serve ourselves and our communities better by making the best choices we can based on the limited information that we have in any given moment. It's up to us to decide why we act, whom we work with, and which risks are worth the lessons and payoffs that we seek. While there are unique challenges to doing purpose-driven work in for-profit contexts, there are also expansive opportunities to test ideas, build generative relationships, and redefine entire fields of practice.

# Embrace the Hustle

For some people, the term "hustle" conjures images of grifters manipulating their marks or start-up bros monetizing our data between in-office Ping-Pong matches. In the mostly white, mostly male world of tech startups and large corporations, "hustling" has become a mantra for performative workaholism rebranded as mission and culture. In the word's first few centuries of use, a "hustle" could mean a game, various forms of literal and figurative pushiness, sex work, grifting, and draft-dodging.[16] It became a dance phenomenon in the 1970s, and more recently, "hustla" has become a self-descriptor for artists like Jay-Z, 50 Cent, and Cassidy. As Isabella Rosario writes for National Public Radio, "Black rappers made hustling cool, weaving it into a narrative about black resilience and self-empowerment. But importantly, their lyrics acknowledged that hustling was what black people needed to do to survive in a rigged system. . . . As with so many concepts that black rappers have made cool, corporations saw an opportunity to cash in on the term and distance it from blackness."[17]

The connection between hustling, agency, and economic prosperity in music culture has its roots in what David Farber calls "street capitalism," the expansion of crack as a business, culture, and epidemic during the Reagan era. As he writes, "the story of crack is also a history of neoliberalism and its cousin, economic globalization, from the ground up." In an environment where "entrepreneurial risk-taking was celebrated" but so-called pathways to the American Dream were closed off to many Black people, "the crack industry was a lucrative enterprise for the self-made men . . . who were willing to do whatever it took to improve their lot in life."[18] Those who excelled in their enterprises became symbols of possibility for musicians and their audiences. "In hip-hop circles, these men often served as underground heroes in a racist society that left too many black men with too little dignity and too few opportunities for exuberant economic success."[19]

Entrepreneurship has historically provided a pathway for people whom capitalism works against to create their own professional and economic opportunities. In *Continually Working*, Crystal Marie Moten shows how the Black beauticians Mattie Pressley DeWese and Mary Evelyn Williams used the tools of entrepreneurship differently to resist racist policies and advocate for economic justice in postwar Milwaukee. Moten writes, "At a time when most Black working women toiled in low-paying positions, beauty work provided a measure of economic autonomy, giving women an opportunity to give back to their community and thus fulfill their desire to be a 'credit' to their city, state, and nation."[20] Entrepreneurship continues to provide avenues for many people operating within rigged systems to find and create opportunities.

Academics and social entrepreneurs alike have critiqued the glorification of the hustle. Weighing the pros and cons of "the neoliberal turn," Lester K. Spence writes that "we no longer respect the dignity of labor, and increasingly propose hustling to make ends meet."[21] Shaw proposes remedies for what she calls "the perils of hustle culture," advocating for community as a force against toxic pressures in the corporate world: "Personally, I feel better just knowing that other people who I look up to also share my bad habits of social comparison and self-criticism."[22] While Spence and Shaw share concerns about how the ways we think about work damage the fabric of our society, Denise Duffield-Thomas insists instead that working long hours is inefficient. Coining the term "chustle (chilled hustle)," she advises, "Just do the things that matter and leave everything else. If you want to make more money, you have a choice: work harder, or leverage everything in your life and make it easier."[23]

For me, hustling is *not* about disrupting for disruption's sake, playing "who will stay in the office latest," or pretending that our systems aren't broken. It is about making the best choices you can in an imperfect world and finding joy in the process. It's about leveraging curiosity and relationships to figure out how to grow something that you care about and pay your rent at the same time. It's not surprising to me that many women I meet, and especially women in the humanities, have a visceral negative response to "entrepreneurship." The business icons we see in the media are mostly white men who make a show of moving fast, breaking things, and making money. As bell hooks wrote, women "are taught via consumerism to believe that they work solely out of material necessity or scarcity, not to contribute to society, to exercise creativity, or to experience the satisfaction of performing tasks that benefit oneself as well as others."[24] We're being told on loop that entrepreneurship isn't for us.

You don't have to be the next Elon Musk to build a successful business that works for you. In fact, if you are skeptical of the trappings of entrepreneurship, chances are that you will approach the design of your business more intentionally than many founders and gravitate toward leaders who share your values. As you move forward, realize the power of building a business on your own terms and the considerable contribution that you are making to the world. I embrace the term "hustle" to signify that it's okay to take pride in our work and to take agency over the moves that we make in our professional lives. To hustle is to recognize the value of what you have to offer and communicate that value externally. In doing so, you reclaim the agency to determine your own path and priorities.

Taking agency over your business means deciding whom you want to work with, what you want to offer, and how you will prioritize time and resources. These skills will not only save you time and headaches as your venture grows but also help you build resilience and crucial skills that you can apply to any future professional opportunities you choose to pursue. Entrepreneurs, too, do best when the act of creation is driven by curiosity, self-reflection, and continuous recalibration of the processes that serve us best. Lenny Cassuto and James Van Wyck emphasize the vital importance of agency in graduate work with a telling metaphor: "These principles [for doctoral advising] should focus more on the agency of the advisee, who is the CEO of their own graduate education."[25] You have the capacity and the agency to design the life you want to have. The principles of entrepreneurship can help you get clear on what you want to achieve and how to leverage your many strengths.

Building systems for sustainable change takes savvy, determination, and the resources to invest in your long-term success. It requires continuous learning and the conviction in your capacity to thrive that can only be gained by trying, stumbling, and course correcting many times over. Only when you build the confidence and competencies to advocate for yourself can you build the complicated solutions required to address the challenges that matter to you.

# Design Better Systems in Community

Within the landscape of social enterprise, there are many emerging philosophies and frameworks that seek to balance the need to make money with the legitimately concerning hypercapitalism of start-up culture. This reality first clicked for me at Entrepreneurship Immersion Week 2022, a conference organized by entrepreneurship@UBC, where Shaw

## 18 HUSTLES FOR HUMANISTS

was a keynote speaker. Shaw is a serial entrepreneur best known as the cofounder of Aisle, a start-up and registered B Corporation that provides sustainable period products. The price of these products reflects a business model rigorous in its attention to climate and social justice: Aisle has invested in life-cycle analysis to track the sustainability of its products from the sourcing of materials through production and shipping as well as customer use, reuse, and disposal. Shaw and her colleagues have invested in long and expensive processes of obtaining Food and Drug Administration approval to ensure that their products are healthy for consumers, for example, by not suffusing plastic particles into our bloodstreams. They have also taken the time, energy, and cost to become certified as a B Corporation, a designation that requires years of staff time to evaluate internal protocols and meet criteria in areas of environmental sustainability and treatment of workers.[26]

At Shaw's keynote speech, she received a question from the audience that she had clearly fielded many times before. "Given that your mission is to make these products accessible, how can you justify charging so much for a pair of panties?" Shaw carefully explained the long road to women's rights in this area, detailing the hard-fought and embarrassingly recent legislation to remove taxes from menstrual products in British Columbia. "Period products should be free, not cheap," she concluded, before emphasizing the collective responsibility of businesses, policy makers and consumers to build more equitable systems.

There has never been a riper or more critical time for humanists to embrace entrepreneurship. Recent history has changed the conversation about how the humanities (and, by extension, humanists) serve society. The pandemic exacerbated inequalities around the world, forcing conversations about access to health care, education, and other basic amenities. It also changed the way we work and connect, challenging long-held assumptions and conventions surrounding what professional life should look like, widening the divide between those who could and couldn't work from home, and shaking up the labor market. Meanwhile, the murder of George Floyd drew attention to systemic racial injustice and mobilized support for the Black Lives Matter movement. Dialogues about how we do better are permeating not only the social sector but also industry, from grassroots social enterprises to the boardrooms of major corporations.

As in Plato's Prometheus myth, the emerging solution in the for-profit world is better governance to help us use the tools we have in ways that don't burn our world to the ground. We see echoes of this narrative in the ways that industry organizations have begun reaching for new ways to contribute to social and climate justice. The philanthropic models of Carnegie and Rockefeller have evolved over the past century through various iterations of what it means to "do good," shifting from a model of charitable heroism to new frameworks intended to be more inclusive and collaborative. The advent of the United Nations Sustainable Development Goals has initiated a shift across industries to more creative thinking around business design for social impact. Environmental, social, and governance (ESG) is trending across corporations that are newly accountable to their customers and shareholders to measure and report on how their companies are creating better outcomes for people and the planet. More and more businesses are actively taking on the rigorous assessments required to become B Corporations, which requires demonstrating a positive track record for everything from carbon footprint to treatment of employees. As not-for-profits increasingly consider new business models to support their operations, the social sector is becoming a more vibrant and creative ecosystem.

These new iterations of social enterprise offer much that humanists can get behind. Many businesses are beginning to reimagine what it means to drive social impact by leveraging the tools we hold most dear: creativity, curiosity, and empathy.

# Enjoy the Process

In his *Book of Delights*, Ross Gay describes delight as "being of and without at once. Or: joy."[27] Unlike pleasure, joy requires our full knowledge of darkness so that we can appreciate light. This, for me, is the essence of being an entrepreneur. I have come to relish the gut-twisting anticipation of risking a thousand minor failures for the chance to create something new. Getting paid is validating, solving problems is satisfying, and it feels nice to receive external validation through payments, client referrals, and social media likes. I hope that my business will be the thing that I do forever, and these conventional metrics help me determine my strategy to make that possible. The pursuit of light makes it worthwhile.

Your business is not a destination—it's a compounding of moments, decisions, and relationships that shape you and the world around you. Every first that you have is worthy of notice and celebration. Signing your first client. Receiving your first thank-you note. Launching your website, your newsletter, your program, or whatever it is that you bring into the world. When things move fast, it's even more important to find moments of stillness to locate yourself. I will never forget the feeling I had when I arrived at the 2022 Princeton GradFUTURES Forum, my first high-stakes, in-person gig after launching a business midpandemic. My wish for you is that you can capture the feeling I had the night before my first live, paid workshop, when I sneaked into the empty lecture hall to project my voice into the void.

You don't have to decide yet (or ever) whether your business is a short-term experiment or a lifelong commitment. As you choose your next steps, I encourage you to know your strengths, celebrate your wins, and live your story on your terms. As you discover new ways to create value for your clients, you may just find that entrepreneurship is the greatest runway your intellectual curiosity has ever seen.

# How to Use This Book

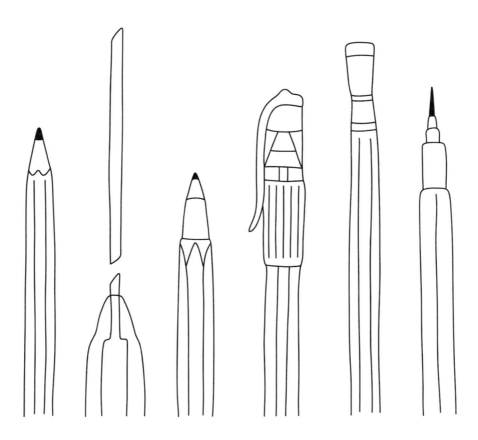

# 22  HUSTLES FOR HUMANISTS

*Hustles for Humanists* shows humanities PhDs and like-minded scholars how to leverage the core competencies they already have, discover new opportunities, fill their knowledge gaps, and bring value to new contexts. This book translates concepts and methods from entrepreneurship into accessible language and strategies that help the reader develop a tailored, actionable plan. The core principles underlying this book are straightforward: recognize your strengths, recognize strengths in others, and leverage curiosity, empathy, and storytelling to create shared value. The chapters that follow show you how to put those principles into practice using the methods, tools, and vocabulary of social enterprise. Each chapter offers strategic advice, examples, and exercises to help you apply the learnings to your own work.

This book is, fundamentally, a resource to help intellectually curious people translate their skills and values to the language of new contexts so that they can discover professional pathways that offer economic stability, the agency to make choices, and joy. Its purpose is to give people who think deeply about the value of humanity the tools to advocate for themselves and for each other. Through the chapters that follow, you will:

- Identify and reframe your professional strengths

- Translate your skills into services

- Negotiate pricing and foster client relationships

- Plan and implement your marketing strategy

- Decide how you want to grow

This book is not a resource for definitive legal or accounting advice, nor is it a roadmap for the "hockey stick" growth so popular in start-up incubators. This book is an act of affirmation, solidarity, and mentorship for humanists who wish to build effective and sustainable enterprises of any size. Most of the examples and anecdotes focus on what is often called "knowledge work." This focus is due, in part, to my own domain of expertise as well as my knowledge and lived experience of common trajectories of ad hoc entrepreneurship in the humanities. Many of the principles I share also apply to product-based businesses and not-for-profits.

This book includes optional exercises, prompts, and references to guide you through your own entrepreneurial journey. It is designed to help you clarify your questions and reflect on your strengths as we begin our work together. Feel free to annotate these pages or write your responses in a separate notebook. You do not need to complete the exercises in linear order. Feel free to return to the prompts whenever you like to deepen your reflections. Take what works for you and leave the rest.

# A Field Guide That Meets You Where You're At

## *For Readers with "No Experience"*

One of my goals in the chapters that follow is to convince you that you have more experience than you think you do. Even if you've never had a client and are just dipping your toe in, this book is designed to help you integrate entrepreneurial principles into your career plan, whether that means starting a business or positioning yourself for job opportunities in new contexts (or both). You may find that some of the exercises in this book are more relevant for your context than others. If you don't have a client, service, or career goal in mind just yet, I encourage you to treat the exercises offered here as thought experiments to reframe the ways you approach your strengths and your network. If a particular exercise is less useful in your current moment, you can always set it aside and revisit it when you're ready.

## *For Active Freelancers*

If you have a business of any kind, this book offers you a framework and exercises to make it more intentional and rewarding. You, too, are free to skim and skip around and locate the lessons and exercises that meet you in your current moment. I encourage you to skim the book as a whole and, perhaps, mine the launch plan in chapter 5 for "low-hanging fruit" exercises that can help you build momentum and start putting the learnings throughout this book into practice. Feel free to review targeted sections when you're ready to revisit your pricing, meet with a new client, sharpen your offer, or launch a new marketing campaign.

### *For Graduate Student Advocates*

Faculty advisors, career development professionals, and professional associations will find in this book resources, exercises, and new ways of framing the role of entrepreneurship in the career trajectories of graduate students and postdocs. The book is designed to complement existing graduate career books and tools like Imagine PhD with targeted advice about how these resources can be adapted for early-career readers interested in exploring entrepreneurship. Many of you have your own side gigs as coaches, speakers, and consultants, and I hope that this book also helps you understand more deeply the value that you offer and the ways that entrepreneurship can help all of us situate our value in context.

# Keywords and Core Concepts

All businesses, from side hustles to global corporations, have at least one thing in common: they need to make money. The language of business offers many frameworks to label and categorize the many other dimensions that most organizations (even solo ones) need to function well. This book is going to introduce you to some vocabulary to help you think of your business as a system and make more efficient use of resources such as banks, accountants, lawyers, and small-business support organizations.

As a starting point, let's review three terms that capture the three pillars of any business: "business operations," "marketing and sales," and "human resources." These pillars will serve as reference points throughout the book to help you synthesize what you learn and integrate the exercises into your own business planning.

*Business operations*: the many pragmatic considerations that enable you to deliver your services and collect payments. Concrete tasks like registering your business, doing your taxes, writing contracts, and paying your bills all fall under this category. The more you organize your processes and paperwork in the early stages of your business, the better prepared you will be to seize opportunities and save yourself time in the long run.

*Marketing and sales*: many forms of storytelling and relationship building that can be simplified or expanded according to your goals and bandwidth. This can be as simple as sending a note to someone in your network to follow up on a potential project, or it can be as complicated as mounting a multiplatform social media campaign to advertise your product or service. Most business owners struggle to develop a balanced marketing strategy, and most marketing strategies evolve alongside internal strengths and external trends. As you craft your own story, this pillar of your business will help you find your voice, clarify your value, and build confidence to pursue new opportunities.

*Human resources*: all things people in your business. Even if you are running the show on your own, I encourage you to think of every investment you make in your own professional development as an HR contribution to your business. By reading this book, for example, you are building capacity for yourself and any future members of the business you are building to work that much more effectively. If you choose to build a team down the road, this pillar will come to include practices like hiring, firing, supporting your employees' learning opportunities, and fostering professional community in the workplace.

# Find Your Inner Entrepreneur

## *Draw from Your Experience*

Why do you want to be a business owner? Entrepreneurship is a tough road, and it requires knowing not only what you want your *business* to *do* but also why *you* want to *do it*. Most of the humanist freelancers I've known began by picking up jobs that crossed their paths to help a colleague out with a project and make a bit of money on the side. Money is seldom the sole motivator that keeps humanists on the entrepreneurial track. Those of us who maintain businesses over time are often motivated by one or more of the following factors:

*Agency*: it can be empowering to choose what you want to work on with whom

*Recognition*: it feels good to know that your contributions are valued by clients

*Networking*: referrals from a happy client can rapidly expand your professional circle

*Flexibility*: choosing your hours and location is nice for some and critical for others

*Curiosity*: running a business opens you up to a never-ending sea of learning opportunities

While these considerations are critical to your personal and professional life, they are not substitutes for being able to pay your rent, feed your family, secure good health care, and enjoy a sense of ease.

Question 1. What does "entrepreneurship" mean to you?

Question 2. Why do you want to learn about entrepreneurship?

---

---

Question 3. Do you see yourself as an entrepreneur? Why or why not?

---

---

## Decide What You Want

When you know what you want your professional life to look like, you are better prepared to build a business that enables you to design that life. This information can help you prioritize whom to pursue as clients, how to scope your services, and when to invest energy in networking.

The "Rank Your Priorities" table on the following page includes some of the most common priorities voiced by graduate students and postdocs during workshops I've delivered for the American Council of Learned Societies, City University of New York PublicsLab, the Princeton Grad-FUTURES Forum, the University of British Columbia Arts Amplifier, and the University of California–Irvine Humanities Center. Use the table to reflect on the factors that are most and least important to you in your professional life. Rank these factors from highest priority (1) to lowest priority. Notice if there are factors that matter to you missing from this list, jot them down, and include them in your rankings.

This exercise is a point of entry into deeper self-reflection and career planning. For more expansive exploration of your skills and values, I recommend starting with Imagine PhD, a free assessment tool and resource repository powered by the Graduate Career Consortium.[1] In *Work Your Career: Get What You Want from Your Social Science or Humanities PhD*, Jonathan Malloy and Loleen Berdahl offer a wealth of reflection exercises and narratives from PhDs who have followed many different career

# Rank Your Priorities

| Factor | Ranking (1 = highest priority) |
| --- | --- |
| Maximum possible income | |
| Alignment of work with personal values | |
| Potential to develop professional relationships | |
| Creative control | |
| Confidence in work quality | |
| Access to learning opportunities | |
| Geographic location or remote work | |
| Team environment | |
| Health insurance and benefits | |
| Other | |

trajectories. Chris Caterine provides more succinct action items in *Leaving Academia: A Practical Guide*.[2] While *Hustles for Humanists* shares with the creators of these resources an emphasis on the value of your skills and the importance of clarifying your values, this book focuses specifically on how you can apply the tools of entrepreneurship to your professional life.

## *How to Set Goals without Crushing Your Spirit*

I am one of those weirdos for whom articulating short-, medium-, and long-term goals is useful and, if you can believe it, fun. For me, it's not so much about choosing a target and then gearing every atom of my being toward that target. Instead, I enjoy imagining my best life and then considering whether the things I am doing right now are aligned with where I want to go. If you find that kind of thinking about your future useful, I invite you to pause here and draw or sketch what you want your life to look like in one, three, and five years. If you don't, bear with me.

I have learned through years of working with faculty and graduate students that, at least within the academy, tagging goals to rigid timelines and metrics can lead many people to spiral with anxiety. This is one of the areas where my research-impact work and career-development work intersect the most. Just as scholars designing seven-year timelines for their grant proposals balk at idea that they can lock their futures into a diagram of dots and arrows, so too early-career humanists resist plotting their futures on what feels like a straight line. For some, the immensity of planning so far ahead can trigger fear of failure. For others, the rigidity of conventional goal setting stifles creative freedom.

I get it. When I was applying to graduate school, I had only the vaguest sense of what the day-to-day work of graduate school would look like, let alone what the job of being a professor actually entails. I knew I liked writing, Chaucer, and my professors, and getting paid to read books instead of paying tuition sounded pretty great. Once in graduate school, the predetermined track of course work, then comprehensive exams, then the steps required to complete a dissertation made goal setting feel unnecessary. On paper, it seemed like my colleagues and I all had exactly the same goals, leading to the same desired outcome: the tenure track. I assumed

## 30 HUSTLES FOR HUMANISTS

that I would land a tenure-track job, and the "track" from there—teach classes, publish book, get tenure—was both prescribed and dependent on the whims of the market. Why, then, bother with setting goals?

Here's what I tell my grant-writing clients who resist setting goals: mapping out your future on your terms is an opportunity to reflect on what you want now, and it helps future you make decisions about whether the ways you spend your time and resources are true to your values. Imagine, for example, that you set a goal to submit your book proposal by one year from now. Six months from now, you'll be in a position to ask yourself the following:

- What steps have I taken to meet my one-year goal?

- Is my one-year goal still my key priority? Why or why not?

- If my one-year goal is still my priority, what do I need to do to make it happen?

- If my priorities have shifted, how can I reorient my actions to realign with my best life?

These reflections will guide you to a key question that Berdahl and Malloy pose in *Work Your Career*: "Given both my future goals and the information currently available to me, what is my best decision right now?"[3] As you gather new information, you will make new choices.

The second case I make to clients for setting goals is this: articulating clear goals for yourself also makes it easier to communicate those goals to others. In the grant world, this means that the people making decisions about whom to fund can picture the future value of your project. Reviewers know as well as you do that research evolves and that it wouldn't be research if you knew the outcomes before you did the work to answer the questions. Part of what they are evaluating is whether you can think through how to solve a problem. It is important that the people in a position to advocate for you know where you want to go and how you see yourself getting there.

I should point out here that many of the goals I articulated for Hikma in October 2020 are totally different from the things I chose to prioritize in October 2021, let alone three years later. In the first months of Hikma, for instance, I thought that the key to my business would be creating a massive social media presence and selling online courses to thousands of people. I quickly learned that I am much better at selling tailored courses to clients I know and like, and shifting to that approach has enabled me to make more money with way less stress. Those relationships have helped me build my credibility to sell open courses without spending hours per week on X and the Metaverse. I've found a way to make a living teaching what I love, but the path I took to get there has been anything but dots and arrows.

## Create Space to Thrive

When I started working from home in March 2020, there was a period of a month or so when the massive construction site across the street temporarily paused its operations. For this brief spell, I started my morning watching from my office window as bald eagles swooped down to use half-built water features as giant birdbaths. As the construction picked up and the magic of remote life grew dull, I struggled to figure out when to stop working, when to go to bed, and how not to binge *Tiger King* a second time. I was, theoretically, working a nine-to-five day job, but those boundaries eroded quickly. The work was still interesting, but being managed by a supervisor who was herself overwhelmed and overtaxed left me feeling underappreciated and frustrated. I started to miss the creativity and flexibility of my dissertation-writing days.

I started Hikma in October 2020, around the time people started referring to pandemic life as "the new normal" and those of us lucky enough to have remote-possible jobs settled into work from home for the long haul. I did three things that, in retrospect, have been as important to my business as any client contract or marketing strategy. First, I moved my desk ninety degrees counterclockwise and three feet to the left. The eagles were long gone, the construction site I had been facing was a daily annoyance, and I preferred the wall newly behind me as the background for my Zoom calls. Second, I forced myself to leave my apartment every day, atmospheric rivers be damned. On days that I knew were going to

 **WRITING PROMPT**

# A Time You Took a Risk

Everyone experiences different risks, and for the most part, we experience risk differently. Think about a risk you've taken recently, big or small. Consider the following:

What were the stakes?

When and why did you take this risk?

What was the outcome?

How did you feel before, during, and after?

*Why this prompt:* Entrepreneurship brings with it different types of risk and uncertainty. How much money will you make next year? Will the client say "yes" to your proposal? Will your idea work?

Early in your entrepreneurial process, it is important to consider your current exposure to different kinds of risk and your level of comfort introducing new risks into your life. Some of these risks have to do with financial security and your ability to flourish in the long term. Others relate to day-to-day choices that business owners make on the fly, often with limited information. Your approach to risk will inform your approach to entrepreneurship.

be long and demanding, that walk included a trip to the local bakery for a takeaway coffee. Third, I set up recurring calendar invitations for phone calls with old friends and family game nights. In retrospect, those touch points are the reason that I still have a business.

Why, you ask, am I telling you about my caffeine habit and interior decorating choices? Because thriving as an entrepreneur requires more than a sound business strategy. In the early days of Hikma, I met an older start-up bro who claimed, with obvious pride, that he had mentored Elon Musk. He gave me the following advice: "You can't be expecting to run a successful business and go taking walks in the afternoon—you have to be prepared to hammer away at it nonstop. No distractions." Friends, this is terrible advice. Boss life can be extremely isolating if you let it. Not letting it requires conscious effort on your part to create space for creativity, reflection, and joy in your daily life.

After years of finding my rhythm as a business owner, I've found many different ways to create space for creativity, balance, and motivation in my business. The little figure pictured on the following page is a Daruma Doll that I picked up at a local market in Vancouver. As the artist who made it explains, it is a Buddhist-based relic designed to support "personal goal setting reminders of dedication and perseverance."[4] Mine has kept me company since I started this book, which is when I circled its left eye in hot-pink chalk. I am looking forward to circling the second eye when I submit my finished manuscript. This ritual is one way that I have made my physical space my own and let my creativity run a little wild.

Sophia van Hees, founder of Brave Snail Designs, writes in her blog that rituals, unlike routines, "focus on the experience itself" and foster a "playful mindset." As we dive in, take a few minutes to start a ritual or identify the ones you are already practicing. Make some tea, go for a walk, take a nap, or do something else to spark your sense of wonder.[5] You'll see from Sophia's art throughout this book how much beauty and creativity are possible when you design your business your way.

We'll talk a lot about celebrating your wins in the chapters that follow. For our purposes, your first win happened the second you cracked open this book. Celebration matters not only in big treats for big milestones but also as a way of creating space for yourself to thrive. As you settle in for the

Daruma doll

ride, take the time to figure out what you need to sustain yourself moving forward. Think about the rituals you already have in place and, if necessary, invent some new ones. Schedule reminders for yourself or, better yet, find like-minded peers who can cheer you on and hold you accountable.

## Chapter Roadmap

The chapters that follow are designed to help you build the thing you want to build the way you want to build it. Throughout these chapters, you will find templates, examples, references, and checklists to make the nuts and bolts of building your business more manageable. Very little is linear in the early stages of entrepreneurship, and I encourage you to take what you need from this book in the order that works best for you. Each chapter focuses on discrete but related strategies for you to tap into as you take your next professional steps.

Chapter 2, "Translate Your Strengths into Services," shows you how to recognize your strengths and translate them into services that you can market and sell. It invites you to identify a service you could offer to a client by tomorrow and to articulate clearly how and to whom you would provide this offer. It then guides you to recalibrate the value of your labor by considering what you bring to the table from the perspectives of potential customers.

Chapter 3, "Name Your Price," provides an overview of some of the most common pricing structures for freelancers who provide services such as writing, editing, indexing, and translating. It reframes pricing as a form of communication and steps through the benefits and limitations of common pricing models.

Chapter 4, "Connect with Your Clients," shows you how to use curiosity, empathy, and communication to build trust-based relationships with your clients. It provides guidance on how to keep yourself open to new opportunities, address conflicts, and advocate for yourself and your business.

Chapter 5, "The Low-Key Launch Plan," provides a step-by-step plan to help you design and implement a low-key launch in twelve weeks. It integrates exercises from the previous chapters with the core language and categories of a typical business proposal. You will be prompted to tell your story in new ways, get your house in order, test new ideas, and reach out to potential clients.

Chapter 6, "Grow Your Own Way," concludes the book by underscoring the importance of community to your success as an entrepreneur and providing prompts to build your own mentorship network.

# 2
# Translate Your Strengths into Services

How many colleagues in your orbit take on side gigs such as editing, translating, or tutoring? There is a common narrative that I observed as a graduate student and have seen play out again and again through professional development work. Many graduate students and recent PhDs pick up freelance work because of a combination of financial precarity and genuine interest. Often, the opportunity emerges when an advisor, a colleague, or a friend from college reaches out for short-term support with a specific project, such as an academic manuscript index, a dissertation copyedit, or a college-bound teenager's personal essay. The ad hoc freelancer accepts the offer, excels, and stumbles into a growing side hustle without any marketing at all.

From an entrepreneurial perspective, being sought after in this way is a strong sign that there is a market for your services. Many humanists in this position, however, lack the clarity, confidence, and language to advocate for themselves as business owners. Once you recognize the true value of your services, you will be well positioned to ask for what you want and seek out the opportunities that work best for you.

This chapter prompts you to translate your strengths into services. Leveraging the strengths-based framework that underpins the book as a whole, it encourages you to take stock of what you already bring to the table and unpack the complexity of your skill set so that you can clarify what you want to offer and communicate the value of that offer to clients. This act of translation moves in both directions, and the chapter defines and situates key vocabulary from the world of entrepreneurship to clarify core business concepts. This chapter builds the foundation for further discussion in the chapters that follow about pricing your offer, developing client relationships, and launching your business. Through the lessons and exercises provided, you will learn to:

- Draft your value proposition

- Clarify your core offer

- Design a tiered scope of work

# Build Your Business on Purpose

I had heard so much about ImaginePhD while writing this book that I decided to try it out for myself.[1] I was shocked and delighted by the results of my Skills Assessment. More than three years after launching my business, my lowest skill scores were in the job family "Entrepreneurship." The results were determined by my own categorization of entrepreneurship-related skills as the ones where I "have more experience . . . but still need guidance." For me, it was a welcome reminder that I, like so many humanists I know, love my job because it lets me learn and grow in the ways that I want to. The flexibility to chart my own path and build relationships through the process is what makes founder life so rewarding.

My encounter with ImaginePhD dovetails with the findings of my research partner, Andrea Webb, through qualitative interviews with students in Hikma's summer 2021 Entrepreneurship for PhDs course. Over the six weeks of this course, I brought together eleven PhD candidates and recent graduates to think through together how to leverage their experiences as emerging scholars for future career steps. Some participants were actively starting businesses or nonprofit organizations. Others were seeking employment opportunities or simply looking for inspiration. Through interviews with participants after the course ended, Webb teased apart the intangible elements of the graduate student experience that are so critical to our professional development but often unacknowledged. As she writes, "While skills and competencies are part of doctoral training, the whole doctoral experience cannot be reduced to a list of competencies."[2] Webb's research indicates that professional agency and participation in communities of practice are vital to the development of academic identities.

I've always thought that the moment when one becomes a scholar is when they transition from the first-year-seminar bravado of "I know everything" to the more reflective "I now know enough to appreciate what I can contribute and just how much I will never know." Great entrepreneurs follow a similar trajectory. Like great scholars, their sharpening awareness of their own specialization enables them to enrich entire fields and communities of practice. It makes little sense, then, that we are

## 40  HUSTLES FOR HUMANISTS

conditioned to believe that needing to learn things is an inherent deficit in our professional value. When that awareness leads you to focus on our limitations, you miss the point: your ability to understand what you need to learn and then fill those gaps is a huge value add for any employer or client. When reframed with self-awareness and intention, your curiosity can be the greatest strength that you offer to your clients.

## *Beware of the Accidental Side Hustle*

Like so many talented humanities professionals, Max has become a victim of their own success. Many graduate students and early-career PhDs pick up some form of freelance work to supplement their income, build relationships, or do a colleague a favor. It starts when a friend or colleague requests "just in time" services such as editing a dissertation, indexing a book, or subbing in for a lecture. These opportunities grow out of relationships built on professional recognition that the skills being offered have value. They often come up because of economic necessity, such as a stopgap between grants, or because the scholar/freelancer has pursued an interesting path and discovered a need or challenge that they are well prepared to address.

Freelancers who find work in these ways are often so skilled that new clients seek them out. As a business owner, it is a great advantage to excel so much at what you do that people will look to you as the person who can solve their problem. Many start-up founders spend years trying to identify "product-market fit," the alignment between the thing one wants to sell and the customers who might someday buy it. Some never do. For many freelancing scholars, however, this also means that you skip the market-research steps that position you to negotiate for a fair rate.

People who can write and teach and give thoughtful answers to difficult questions possess a rare skill set that is sought after across industry, government, and the social sector. If your services are selling themselves, this means that your value is already visible to at least one customer and compelling enough that they are willing to pay for it. You have already vaulted one of the greatest hurdles that stops other start-ups before they

◇◇◇◇◇◇◇◇◇◇◇◇◇◇◇◇◇ **SCENARIO** ◇◇◇◇◇◇◇◇◇◇◇◇◇◇◇◇◇

# The Success Spiral: Max the Digital Creative

The pandemic hit just as Max committed to a 4/4 course load, a condition of their postdoctoral fellowship. With safety protocols in flux, Max developed creative approaches to digital learning that allowed for remote, in-person, and hybrid teaching. They discovered a passion for digital media creation that led to excellent teaching evaluations, engaging standalone content, and a bit of a following among the university's Center for Digital Learning (CDL) network. This attention has led to requests for digital media services, including an invitation to produce the CDL's new podcast.

Max takes on the podcast project with gusto. Through a series of emails, Max and the CDL director agree that Max will edit eight recordings into episodes for the first season. Based on Max's previous experience, they anticipate that each episode will take about six hours. A week later, the CDL director writes to Max asking whether Max knows of possible guest interviewees with expertise in the area. Max knows several great candidates and offers to put them in touch with the director.

Requests from Max's new client quickly begin to snowball. They ask Max to schedule and attend the recordings, draft interview questions, and manage the CDL's rigorous consent and archival processes. When Max edits and submits the first episode, the director asks them to cut twenty minutes and provide show notes and a transcript. Could Max also comb the free libraries for appropriate music and splice it in? The director is sorry to ask, but they simply don't have time.

What should Max do?

◇◇◇◇◇◇◇◇◇◇◇◇◇◇◇◇◇◇◇◇◇◇◇◇◇◇◇◇◇◇◇◇◇◇◇◇◇◇◇◇◇◇◇

have even begun. Don't sell yourself short by failing to think through your value and skills.

There are two sides to the "accidental side hustle" coin. Stumbling into freelance work is a strong sign that one other person already sees at least one dimension of your value. Ad hoc requests with one-time payments are valuable indicators that there is greater value under the surface. Too many freelancers see these opportunities as favors from their clients instead of value offered to them. If you are someone who has picked up ad hoc freelance work fueled solely by word of mouth, take heart in the knowledge that your talents are so clear that, without any intentional selling at all, you have attracted customers and, possibly, grown your business through word of mouth and referrals.

At the same time, when you let others set your terms for you, you relinquish your agency. The danger of letting your services sell themselves is that you miss out on opportunities to cultivate an intentional, strategic system for your business. If you decline to negotiate and ignore what other service providers are charging, you are likely to be underpaid for your labor. If you don't articulate the parameters of an agreement at the outset, clients will breach your boundaries and take more than you were planning to give. No matter the scale of your business, knowing your worth and building an intentional system for yourself will better prepare you to charge what you are worth, collect payments, and predict your future revenue. It will also enable you to understand your business as a constellation of choices, rather than an afterthought you stumbled into to make ends meet.

## Be Your Own Best Advocate

The curiosity that drives us to sit with complicated, ambiguous concepts for months, if not years, builds resilience and rigor that can help you differentiate your hustle from anything else on the market. It will help you craft new questions as your market research unfolds and position the things you learn along the way into a greater framework. When combined, curiosity and empathy will enable you to understand what drives your customers and to build relationships based on mutual respect and reciprocity. Empathy will help you build a community and a professional network to help you answer your questions faster and sustain you when new challenges inevitably emerge. In this chapter, we explore three types of questions that will help you build your business as an intentional system, whether your goal is to build a healthy side hustle or to grow an international corporation.

No matter the scale of your business, knowing your worth and building an intentional system for yourself will better prepare you to charge what you are worth, collect payments, and predict your future revenue. It will also enable you to understand your business as an intentional choice, rather than an afterthought you stumbled into to make ends meet. Many humanities graduates find themselves doing freelance work not because they have actively pursued it but because others have recognized their value as writers, editors, evaluators, and research consultants. The economic realities of graduate school and adjunct life have fostered a system in which many humanities scholars build near-accidental "side hustles" through which they edit dissertations, develop monograph indices, assess student work, and take on other freelance work out of interest mixed with economic necessity.

In this chapter, we approach that discovery process more intentionally by asking readers to imagine or refine a service that they could offer to a client by end of day tomorrow. This emphasis on a narrow scope will serve to demonstrate that humanities professionals have developed complex networks of skills that may bring different forms of value to diverse customers across contexts. The challenge of narrowing to a specific service for a targeted customer will build the scaffolding to reframe one's value in more tangible terms.

The first step to building a viable system for your business is to recognize what you bring to the table. People with years of advanced graduate training often underestimate the value that their skills and experience may bring to other professional contexts. Without the conviction that their services require a unique skill set, many humanities freelancers lack the skills and information to scope their work appropriately and determine a

## 44 HUSTLES FOR HUMANISTS

fair market rate. This chapter draws on case studies and research in business and social innovation studies to contextualize the value of humanities skills in the marketplace. Often, the most effective way to pivot to a new track is not to learn a new skill set but instead to translate what you already know and do for new audiences. The next section dives deeply into the first pillar of this book's strengths-based framework: before pursuing additional training or credentials, recognize and articulate the strengths you already have.

# Know Your Value

Not long ago, a PhD candidate with whom I have worked closely mentioned that she was participating in an entrepreneurship program through her university. She and a couple of colleagues have decided to launch a grant-writing business when they graduate. This colleague played a critical role in helping a faculty member win a competitive, multimillion-dollar grant that required complex planning and coordination. Referring to her counterparts in the tech-focused stream of her program, she said, "They're a lot further than we are, of course." I looked at her skeptically. "No, they're not," I told her. "They just know different words."

As with any form of translation, the repurposing of your academic training for business requires a working knowledge of the key vocabulary. The lingo of "entrepreneurship"—words like "start-up" and "innovation"—can be intimidating to some humanists and eye roll inducing to others. The jargon of the start-up world serves much the same purpose as specialist language in any discipline: it can be used as an effective shorthand or as a tool to exclude the unindoctrinated. While it's not necessary to swallow an MBA textbook to succeed as a business owner, proficiency in some of the core concepts and terms will help you build confidence in your craft and make effective use of existing frameworks and principles. In this chapter, we'll cover three key concepts from the start-up world that will serve you well: the *value proposition*, the *minimum viable product*, and the *scope of work*.

◇◇◇◇◇◇◇◇◇◇◇◇ **WRITING PROMPT** ◇◇◇◇◇◇◇◇◇◇◇◇

# Your First Job

So much of entrepreneurship is about telling your own story. Think about your first job, defining "job" as the first working position where you were compensated for a defined set of responsibilities. You might have worked at a diner, volunteered for a community organization, or helped out a family member with a small business. Respond to the following questions:

- What was the job?
- Why did you choose this job?
- What did you like and dislike about it?
- What's something you learned on the job that you still use today?

*Why this prompt:* Your past work experience offers a window into some of your earliest known transferable skills. It may also provide insights about your career choices, lessons learned, and what matters to you in your professional life. Remembering your earliest experiences of work can help you think more expansively about what you want your professional life to be like and the value that you hope to offer through your business.

My colleague Ai Mizuta shared her experience of her first job working in a donut shop in Japan. She learned to communicate with customers, show up on time, and get along with coworkers. "It was strict, and it gave me very good basics on how to handle difficult people," said Ai. "I feel like I can work anywhere after that job."

## *Think like an Entrepreneur*

Like the humanities graduate school experience, entrepreneurship requires cultivating resilience in the face of uncertainty. Nobody writes a prospectus knowing exactly where their dissertation will go, just as nobody writes a business plan for a new venture knowing that their market will respond as they imagine. We review the literature—or do the market research—to map out the ideas that have been offered and the ways we've received them. Once we have identified the gap in knowledge—or the market—that we will address, we think through the right questions to ask. We recruit mentors to help us understand the problem and the process.

As our ideas grow and change, we continuously recalibrate the elements that matter most to our argument. We learn to sidestep rabbit holes and gradually to invest in the pieces of our work that we know to be our most valuable contributions. The ability of humanities scholars to tolerate uncertainty and keep writing through it is, in my experience, almost unique in the professional landscape.

Entrepreneurs strive to create products and services that don't yet exist. As a scholar, you create knowledge that doesn't yet exist. In both cases, this process involves risk, self-determination, and careful attention to the behavior of those around you.

Be responsive to market needs. While humanists may never actually use the word "pivot" like people in businesses often do, we certainly know how to make a hard turn. The academic context trains us to receive and respond to detailed critiques. When we are faced with three sets of reviewer feedback that seem equally thorough but diametrically opposed, we find the common threads, decide what is useful, and determine the changes that will make our work most compelling to our scholarly audience, or "target market."

When I started my business, many entrepreneurs advised me to steel myself for direct feedback and, specifically, for having ideas that I felt passionate about be shredded and rejected over and over again. That was my first indication that the leap from academe to entrepreneurship might be vaultable.

You should know that you have these competencies, regardless of how you choose to use them. Whether you land a tenure-track position, find your way to a new career path, or launch your own start-up, your core values, resilience, and agility will stay with you. Whatever you decide, make your choices with full knowledge of your competencies as well as recognition of all the things you have left to learn. Use your skills in research and analysis to seek out resources and find your footing in new conversations.

## *Identify Your Value Proposition*

When I taught Writing and Rhetoric to freshmen at the University of Notre Dame, I would tell them that every form of communication is an argument. Every social media post, every image, and every conversation makes implicit claims about your audience, your knowledge base, and what you stand for. As humanists, we learn to iterate on our arguments within evolving conversations where new research is continuously changing the game. Your process and adaptation over time, not to mention the track record that you establish while engaging in these conversations, are the core of your system. Your ability to thrive in contexts of change, uncertainty, and ambiguity is a quality that you share with all successful entrepreneurs.

One of the most valuable concepts for emerging entrepreneurs to master is the "value proposition," a statement that one uses to convey to a customer how the entrepreneur's product or service will benefit that customer. The value proposition is widely understood as a way of capturing why your business exists so that you can design an effective business model and marketing strategy. For example, a professional grants crafter might say to a client, "My grant-writing services will help you submit a compelling proposal on time and with less stress." While the term "value proposition" and the constellation of jargon surrounding it can be intimidating to those who are unfamiliar with industry culture, the concept is intuitive for many humanists.

Let's recontextualize the "value proposition" through humanistic principles of communication, reason, and audience, reframed through the lens of Aristotle's three pillars of persuasion: ethos, pathos, and logos.

48  HUSTLES FOR HUMANISTS

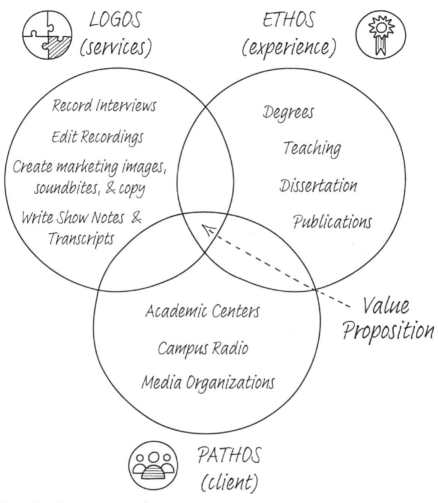

Example value proposition diagram

These pillars simplify the value proposition into its basic rhetorical purpose: to persuade your target client that the thing you are offering will benefit them. These discrete components also enable more effective storytelling, as the reader can choose which components to highlight in a particular context and translate those elements into the most accessible language for a specific audience.

Consider Max's scenario through Aristotle's principles of persuasion.

The concept of the "value proposition" can help us build conceptual common ground between the language of business and the work of humanists. For Max, it provides a framework to connect Max's teaching, creative media experience, and field knowledge with the client's immediate needs. For the immediate opportunity and target client, Max's value proposition might sound something like, "I help academic centers share stories and spark relationships by producing podcasts that delight and inspire listeners." As you seek out new opportunities, refine your value proposition to reflect your deepening understanding of your value to your clients. As your business grows and changes, your value proposition will be useful for building relationships with new clients, partners, and funders.

## *Exercise: Draft Your Value Proposition*

Take few minutes to sketch your own version of this diagram based on what you know now about your skills, experience, and existing or potential clients. As you progress through this chapter, look for inspiration to think more expansively about what you bring to the table and how to communicate the value of your contributions.

What services do you want to offer?

What is your experience?

50  HUSTLES FOR HUMANISTS

Who is your client?

_____

_____

_____

Write a sentence explaining how your service will benefit your client.

_____

_____

_____

# What Humanists Bring to the Table

As I have written for *Inside Higher Ed,* teaching and the dissertation prepare us for so much more than many of us realize.[3] While academic culture trains many of us to treat the PhD like a vocation, it is fundamentally a job. Like any job, it involves a collection of responsibilities for which the employee receives financial compensation. By breaking down those responsibilities into tasks, skills, and competencies, we can collect a set of terms that will be easier to translate for client proposals and job applications alike. The following sections break down teaching and the dissertation into the clusters of skills they represent.

## *Teaching Is a Job*

When I was a graduate student, a career services adviser told me that, if I included teaching on my résumé, a nonacademic employer would assume that the job they were offering was my plan B. That is nonsense.

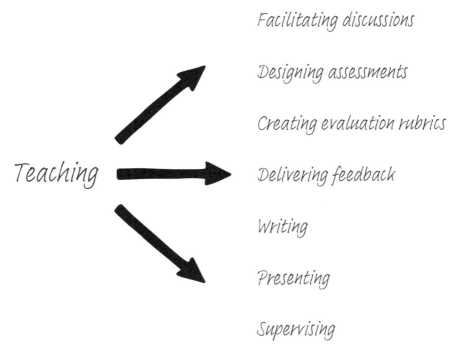

Teaching skills

My teaching experience was by far the most résumé-friendly aspect of my PhD experience. It was also the one that best prepared me to work in a team setting. Designing and delivering a course in the humanities requires planning a long-term project with many moving parts and stakeholders (students). It involves developing robust evaluation plans, tracking the progress of many individuals, coordinating peer groups, conducting assessments and providing critical mentorship.

Being an instructor caused me massive anxiety as a graduate student, because I constantly felt underprepared to present myself as an expert in a conversation that, by my own design, could move in organic and unanticipated directions. Working as a staff member in a central academic office for a number of years, I came to learn that the humanities seminar-style mode of teaching is, in fact, a distinct disciplinary advantage. For example, professional meetings require organization, planning, and active engagement. The drawbacks of ineffective meetings have only been

## 52   HUSTLES FOR HUMANISTS

exacerbated with the necessity of making them virtual, and so the ability to guide a productive discussion has become an even more marketable skill—especially if you have experience teaching online.

The emotional intelligence and flexible thinking involved in teaching a humanities seminar course are difficult to quantify. However, outside of the humanities, I have learned that a word and a role embody these skills: "facilitation." The ability to get a group of people with differing views and experiences to have a productive conversation is vital and surprisingly rare. If PhD candidates can capture that skill in their job materials or business services, it will probably be much more impressive than the "number of students taught."

## *The Dissertation Is a Job*

The "Dissertation" item of my first résumé went something like this: "Wrote a 264-page dissertation. Drew on sources in X, Y, and Z languages. Explored Arabic influences on medieval English literature." That was not an effective hook for potential employers, because it didn't tell them anything about how I would work for them. The dissertation is an idiosyncratic experience, and it is so all-consuming that it can be difficult to examine the process and skills involved from a critical distance.

If you have defended a humanities dissertation, you have defined the scope of a sprawling initiative in consultation with senior colleagues. Project management in the context of professionals who speak the language of project management—"deliverables," "roadblocks," and so forth—is a challenge. Project management as a junior colleague in an academic department—a system of obscure processes, idiosyncratic working habits, and erratic communication—is Everest. You have designed timelines, articulated milestones, and responded to a complexity of feedback the likes of which you may never see again. Name and honor those accomplishments.

Framing the dissertation in terms of its skills can also provide immediate opportunities to practice research communication and build your professional online presence. The ability to distill a chunk of a dissertation into a blog post, op-ed, or even a tweet is a vital and marketable skill.

In many ways, writing a dissertation leads us to the core competencies of entrepreneurship. Once you spot them, you can build an intentional system and position yourself for success in any professional context. Through the daily work that you undertake to develop courses, finish your dissertation, and advocate for yourself, you are practicing core elements of entrepreneurship. The most effective way to translate those skills to new professional contexts is to reframe them as a coherent system through which you offer value. Lay this groundwork during your PhD, and you will be in a much stronger position to find or create meaningful work.

The deeper into the weeds of our specializations we get, the easier it is to forget how much we already know. When you first take stock of your existing strengths and goals, it becomes much easier to filter an endless landscape of skill-development opportunities and focus on the ones that will best prepare you to thrive in your chosen path, whether that's a job, a business, or both.

Addressing these obstacles requires choosing how you want to leverage your strengths. Before you can leverage your strengths, you need to recognize them. Strengths become "services" when you structure, communicate, and apply them in such a way that a client will buy them.

## Look Beyond Your Academic Experience

In *Work Your Career*, Berdahl and Malloy provide useful descriptions of "career competencies" that many emerging scholars develop over the course of their degrees, such as "teamwork," "leadership," and "global and intercultural fluency."[4] I agree with them wholeheartedly that, when positioning yourself for professional opportunities, "Evidence in the form of specific experience and tangible outputs is key."[5] As you take stock of your competencies, don't overlook the wealth of experience beyond and adjacent to your academic work. The expanded version of your "ethos" diagram might actually look something like the one pictured here.

Starting your search for inspiration within the work to which you've devoted most time makes sense. Basalla and Debelius write, "As every graduate student knows, your dissertation topic is a mini-Rorschach test of your personality."[6] By reflecting on both the content of your dissertation

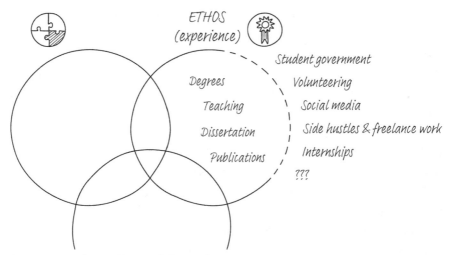

Experience within and beyond the academy

and the process you've created to write it, you can learn a lot about your values and how you design your experience of work for yourself when left to your own devices.

The same is true of the compensated jobs and uncompensated work you take on in addition to your core scholarly responsibilities. When you find the patterns between those activities, you'll be better prepared to articulate what you bring to the table and understand why new opportunities speak to you. Caterine describes the typical trajectory of scholars beginning new careers: "Once you settle into your environment, you'll connect the dots faster, synthesize information with greater ease, and explain complex topics more clearly than people who have more experience but less formal training in the art of learning."[7] In the environment of entrepreneurship, working with clients reveals very quickly how valuable the "art of learning" is to delivering creative and effective services.

## Make These Hustles Your Own

Not sure yet what you want to offer? No worries—here are some ideas to borrow or use as inspiration for your own approach.

*Translation*: Apply your language skills to helping scholars, community organizations, government offices, or other clients make their content accessible and credible for new publics.

*Editorial consulting*: Make your clients' documents reader ready with copyediting or engage with them to shape and refine writing projects from the ground up.

*Tutoring*: Help your clients learn core concepts, build confidence, and ace their courses.

*Content development*: Elevate your clients' marketing strategies with clear and compelling content for websites, blogs, and social media.

*Program evaluation*: Synthesize quantitative and qualitative data about your clients' programs so that they can evaluate their progress, make informed decisions, and build a case for long-term funding.

These ideas are a brief sampling from the many successful ventures that founders in my orbit have launched and developed. If you're still exploring, try on one of these hustles and use it as a thought experiment in the exercises throughout this book.

# Choose What to Offer

Most services in the knowledge economy can be simplified or complicated. Remember Max, our podcast editor whose project quickly snowballed? For Max, in the context of this contract, the lowest-common-denominator service is editing a set number of recordings. We could break this unit down further by clarifying what "editing" means: Is Max shaping the story or simply cleaning up the sound quality? How many rounds of revision will they offer? Are they splicing in additional content, such as the soundtrack?

# 56  HUSTLES FOR HUMANISTS

One dimension of Max's value is the podcast they are helping the CDL create, which will help the client fulfill their mission of supporting the university's teaching and learning community. The director will also benefit from implicit advantages such as a visible "success story" for their office, relationships with the interviewees, and more of that precious, finite resource: time. The director's constant requests for Max to do more indicate that they recognize this value. The question is, Is the client paying for that value?

## *Done Is Better than Perfect*

How many of us have heard the mantra "done is better than perfect" in the final throes of our dissertations? It is easy to get lost in the weeds when you are writing a thesis on, say, postmodern architecture or the gender politics of early science fiction. In my case, I spent two weeks in a windowless room full of rare-book-library catalogs chasing down sources related to a fourteenth-century town/gown brawl at Oxford. For a hot minute, I was convinced that the St. Scholastica Day Riots were the key to connecting chapters that I was struggling to fit together. After months of writing in circles, however, I mostly relegated that content to footnotes and a blog post.[8] By the final stage of writing, looming deadlines forced me to prioritize the ideas that would serve me best in my current moment.

While exploring new questions and directions is an essential part of creating something valuable, so is figuring out which rabbit holes are worth the chase. One of the great joys of entrepreneurship, for me, is being able to test big ideas in smaller bites and gather feedback quickly. For scholars used to polishing work to (near) perfection before putting it out into the world, this can be an uncomfortable process at first. It gets easier with practice and by learning to simplify your services. One critical tenet of early-stage start-ups is that testing the most basic version of your offer enables you to contain the delivery of the offer itself as you learn about your customer and refine your business model. Entrepreneurs have a name for this lowest common denominator: the "minimum viable product" (MVP). The MVP concept is often used in the context of early-stage development of technologies, such as the video game that can "only shoot zombies" or the early testing of Rent the Runway as an in-person dress-rental service.[9] Whether or not you want to build something that you can automate and scale, developing your services incrementally will help you clarify your strategy as quickly and efficiently as possible.

Doing "the minimum" is a tall order for those of us who are used to overachieving and grappling with complex problems over long periods of time. If you can master this approach, however, you will be well positioned to learn faster, collect payments sooner, and design the next steps of your business more intentionally. In *Testing Business Ideas*, David J. Bland and Alex Osterwalder prompt readers to create and test a "Single Feature Minimum Viable Product," which they describe as "a functioning minimum viable product with the single feature needed to test your assumption."[10] They invite readers to share the MVP with customers, gather feedback, and then evaluate the total cost to create the product, customers' satisfaction, and the number of customers who came on board.

## *Identify a Service You Could Offer by Tomorrow*

We'll come back to the process of gathering feedback and evaluating your progress in chapters 5 and 6. For now, let's focus on clarifying the most essential elements of what you want to offer. As Bill Aulet writes in *Disciplined Entrepreneurship*, "Your odds of success are higher if you limit the number of variables in your initial product, getting something that works into the customer's hands quickly even if it does not have all the functionality you would like it to include."[11] The core principles of the minimum viable *product* can also be applied to the service you identified in this chapter's first exercise. Once you clarify your offer, you will have a distilled building block for our discussion of pricing, customer relationships, and testing ideas in the chapters that follow. For the purposes of this book, your "core offer" is the simplest service you are prepared to deliver. By expanding your core offer incrementally, you can control your pace of learning and create more value for your clients over time.

Imagine that a friend or colleague calls you and asks you for a favor—they need something from you, and they need it tomorrow. They are willing to pay. Given your skills and experience, what is that service likely

## 58 HUSTLES FOR HUMANISTS

to be? Whether or not this has happened to you in the past, take a few minutes to reflect on a service you could deliver by tomorrow. To narrow it further, pick something you know how to do and could deliver from start to finish in eight hours or less. Let's call that service your "core offer."

What is your core offer?

 

 

Who is your ideal client?

 

 

If you're feeling stalled, take some inspiration from Max's story. Remember that Max's first project with their client was to edit a single recording into a podcast episode. Some other examples include editing a single chapter of a dissertation, tutoring a friend's kid for an hour, drafting a blog post, or translating a few pages of a text from one language to another.

## *Define Your Scope of Work*

In my first-ever Hikma contract, I agreed that I would "develop" a grant proposal draft for a client. A few weeks later, it became clear that my client and I had very different ideas about what it meant to "develop": Would I do all of the writing? Would I review technical background materials? Would I provide an updated draft every time new feedback came in, as my client expected? How many rounds of revision were reasonable? My future service proposals and contracts took these considerations into account, and the specificity has made it easier to build strong relationships with clients and plan my workload.

The goal of this exercise is to simplify your core offer according to learnings from the MVP approach. Given the limits of the one-day turn-around, you may have a clear idea in your mind of what your core offer looks like. Your client may not share your vision. Detailing your offer as a scope of work enables you to make sure that you and your client have the same expectations for what you will deliver. At minimum, your scope of work should include the following:

- *Description of the offer*: What will you deliver?

- *Timeline*: When will you do it?

- *Price*: What is the cost to your client?

- *Client responsibilities*: What do you need from your client?

Don't worry about pricing your offer for now—we'll get to that in chapter 3. For now, focus on getting as specific as you can about the details of the offer itself. If the offer is time bound, like a tutoring session, make sure to factor in not only meeting time but also preparation or debriefing that provides direct value to the client. If you are editing or translating, try specifying word count as well as the type and complexity of the content. Find the appropriate parameters for your service.

To continue with Max's case, what are the parameters of editing a podcast episode within one day? Max's scope for their core offer looks something like this:

- Max will edit a single podcast episode from a preexisting audio recording of no more than sixty minutes.

- The episode editing service will include sound-quality improvements and minor cuts to remove excess content and improve narrative flow.

- The client will need to provide the recording upon signing of the agreement.

- Max will deliver the final product as a WAV file within five business days.

- The total cost to the client is $500.

**60** HUSTLES FOR HUMANISTS

Even this scope leaves room for ambiguity. For example, who decides which content is "excess"? What constitutes a "minor" cut? The more specific you can get when articulating your scope of work, the better.

## *Exercise: Refine Your Core Offer*

Articulate the following components of your core offer. Take your best guess at the price, and plan to revisit your offer after reading chapter 3.

Description of the offer:

_____

_____

Timeline:

_____

_____

Price:

_____

_____

Client responsibilities:

_____

_____

This core offer is one building block available to you as you decide what you want to offer. As you draft, jot down any additional services that you could offer on top of your core service. Remember to be as specific as possible about the services that you will provide and the outputs that your client will receive. In start-up terms, these outputs are often called "deliverables."

When scoping your work, make sure that the client understands what is *not* included in your offer. In this example, Max might clarify that the service will not include recording the interview, drafting show notes, or adding music to the episode. One easy way to draw those lines is to say that extra services like these are available for an additional fee.

# Expand Your Services

Defining your scope up front makes it easier to protect your boundaries later. Your time is a finite resource, and you deserve to be compensated fairly for good work. When you articulate your scope, you clarify, to the best of your ability, what will and will not be included in your services. Setting these parameters early in the process makes it easier to say no when additional asks creep in (more on that in chapters 3 and 4). If you want the extra work, having a clear scope also makes it easier to say, "Yes, I can do that, and this is what it costs." Equally important for your business, communicating your value and boundaries to your client up front sparks an ongoing conversation about how you will work together.

When you provide your client with a proposal that includes a clear scope of work, you give them the opportunity to ask questions about your approach up front. You, in turn, can adapt in ways that will satisfy everyone's needs and priorities before locking yourself into a particular approach or rate. Even a client who chooses your most basic service option will have a clear understanding of other services that you can offer down the road. This opens the door for future work and strong referrals.

In what remains of this chapter, I invite you to develop a tiered scope of work. You will design services that build iteratively on the core offer

62  HUSTLES FOR HUMANISTS

you identified and refined earlier. For now, the intention behind articulating your services in this way is to help you drill down into your "basic" service so that you can understand how more expansive services call on your strengths and create additional value for your client. Chapter 3 will step through the pros and cons of various pricing models available to you as you decide your rates for these services. Before we get there, keep in mind that pricing your services as bundles of deliverables is often called "project rates," "productizing," or "value-based pricing." This is not the only way to set your prices, but we'll assume for purposes of the following exercise that you will charge project rates.

The best way to lay the groundwork for a smooth and mutually beneficial client engagement is to be as clear and specific as possible up front about what will (and what won't) be included in your services. I find it helpful to offer my potential clients three possible scopes of work for a given project. This process guides me to reflect in advance about how I imagine the work will unfold and to catch any hidden steps or complications that I can anticipate up front. It also enables me to show my clients the layers of complexity involved in delivering different combinations of services. By spelling out the complexity of the work, you can make a strong and tangible case for the value of your offer. When you are very clear from the outset about what you will deliver, you are better prepared to advocate for yourself during every step of your client engagement.

Writing for the *Harvard Business Review*, Rafi Mohammed provides some historical context and tangible examples of what he calls "Good-Better-Best Pricing." Mohammed offers examples of tiered pricing from the automotive industry, gas stations, and even charging for basic and premium cable TV options. In one succinct example, "Car washes typically offer several options, separated by services such as waxing and undercoating." As Mohammed explains, tiered pricing can both expand services for customers to access premium options and make your services accessible without devaluing them: "First, companies can dramatically lift margins by creating a high-end Best version that persuades existing customers to spend more or attracts a new cohort of high spenders. . . . Second, and at the other end of the spectrum, a low-priced Good offering can make a product accessible to price-sensitive or dormant customers."[12] This is a useful alternative to offering deep discounts that undervalue your services.

The "Scope Options" table on the following page lays out for Max the same structure that I use in my own proposals for clients. We'll dive into pricing in chapter 3, and chapter 4 lays out where and when to introduce the scope of work in your negotiation process. For now, let's imagine that Max drafts this document following an initial conversation with their client about the support they are looking for. Notice how each option scaffolds onto the one before it. What is the added value as the scope of work expands?

# Create the Conditions for Shared Value

No matter how carefully you set your boundaries, there will almost certainly be moments when you or your clients cross them. "Scope creep" is the process through which a service provider's commitment to a client extends over time to encompass responsibilities that are not compensated and often not explicitly discussed. A client asks for an extra meeting, an extra edit, or a similar detail that pushes the project a bit beyond what the provider had bargained for. The provider gives the extra, and similar requests quickly come in. Second rounds of editing become third rounds, meetings run longer, and an arrangement that seemed promising is suddenly cutting into other opportunities. When presented with scope creep, you have three choices: say no, give extras, or renegotiate the terms of your agreement. Each of these actions is easier to take when your scope of work is crystal clear. We'll talk more about how to communicate and protect your boundaries in chapter 4.

The positive side of scope creep is that clients who want more from you typically see value in what you are offering, including value beyond what you knew you could contribute. Design your offer for what you want to do and how you want to work. The most creative and expansive projects tend to evolve over time, surfacing new possibilities along the way. As you get to know your clients and test your services on the market, you will

# Scope Options

## Option A: Basic          $

Editing services for eight podcast episodes as follows:
- Edit recordings provided by the client (max. sixty minutes) into audio files of forty to forty-five minutes
- Edit sound quality to reduce background noise and improve tone
- Cut fifteen minutes at the beginning and end of each recording to trim introductions and Q&A
- Provide all edited recordings as WAV files in thirty business days

Client responsibilities:
- Record interviews
- Secure permissions from guest speakers
- Provide all recordings as WAV files the day the agreement is signed

## Option B: Comprehensive          $$$

Option B includes all services in Option A, plus the following:
- Provide one round of additional edits per episode to cut undesired content requested by the client
- Provide transcripts of finalized episodes as TXT files
- Provide brief descriptions of each episode (150–200 words/episode) in a Word document

Client responsibilities:
- Annotate the TXT files provided by Max to indicate where additional cuts should be made
- Publish the transcripts and show notes content on client's website and podcast platform

## Option C: Premium          $$$$$

Option C includes all services in Option B, plus the following:
- Write and design a two-page PDF resource with audio-recording guidelines for guest speakers
- Provide technical support during recording sessions, including sound checks and facilitation
- Provide one draft of a six-hundred-word blog post to accompany each episode as a Word document.
- Produce a two-minute trailer to promote the podcast season
- Provide graphic design of one thumbnail per episode for use on the client's website and social media

Client responsibilities:
- Share documents with and secure permissions from guest speakers
- Host, post, and publish all materials
- Confirm Max's availability before scheduling recordings

figure out how to design your scope to suit your style and goals. Chapters 3 and 4 will help you get there by guiding you to set reasonable rates and manage client relationships. In chapter 3, we'll explore how to set your rates, why to charge what you are worth, and the pros and cons of several common pricing models. Chapter 4 will integrate that guidance on pricing with the work you've done here to clarify your value and communicate your offer to your client. Keep your core offer and value proposition in mind as you work through the rest of this book.

# 3

## Name Your Price

# Pricing Is a Conversation

As I've learned more and more about pricing and negotiation, a few metaphors have surfaced to describe the process of pitching an offer to a client. Pitching is a "magic trick," getting a client to commit is a "dance" or "dating," and leading a client to see the rationale behind your pricing comes down to "storytelling." All of these metaphors have helped me to sharpen my own approach and shift my perspective around pricing and negotiation. There is an art to knowing when to ask questions, when to speak in broader terms, and when to make the leap from theoretical alignment to a negotiation of cash value for the services. Above all these other metaphors, however, I find it useful to frame the process of reaching alignment with clients as a conversation. Negotiation depends on so many contextual factors, of which the dollar amount exchanged is only one of many considerations that determine the value of your work to your client.

In chapter 2, we framed the concept of the "value proposition" through the lens of Aristotle's principles of persuasion. You honed your offer as the point of intersection between your credibility, the product or service you propose to provide, and your client's need. The "value proposition," we said, is the way that you communicate to your client that your offer will benefit them. As your business grows, neither your offer nor your client's needs will remain static. You will get better at delivering your services, and you will probably learn or discover new things that you can offer. You may also find that your services fit a technical niche that is rare and that your subject expertise or specific approach is more valuable to a certain set of clients than similar services they can find elsewhere. At the same time, if you succeed in building strong relationships with your clients, you may receive requests for support beyond what you had imagined you could give.

Chapter 2 invited you translate your strengths into services and choose what to offer. In this chapter, we'll step through how to price those services. You will learn to:

+ Reframe the way you think about money and value

- Calculate your baseline rate

- Price your services using a range of methods

Thinking and talking about money take practice. The exercises in this chapter are designed to help you establish some working parameters that will help you make decisions as a business owner. I suggest that you do these exercises once quickly based on your gut instincts and best guesses and then, when you are ready, take the time to do some research and come back. You can and should return to your answers over time, and you should also discuss them with partners, mentors, and professional experts such as financial planners.

## Why Talking about Money Makes Us Cringe

If you treat your approach to negotiation as an ongoing conversation with your clients, you will learn more about your clients' needs and find new ways to address them. In the language of entrepreneurship, you will find new "solutions" to more specific "problems," honing your negotiation, pricing, and delivery strategies along the way. Talking about money is uncomfortable for many humanists, particularly when we envision our work serving the public good in some way. The idea that the privilege of "doing good" should be reward enough in itself can cripple your capacity to advance and sustain purpose-driven work. If you can't pay your rent, take breaks, or invest in more efficient operations for your business, you will burn out. When you do, your dreams of effecting positive change may well grind to a halt. I suggest reframing money as the tool that enables you to apply your empathy and curiosity to complex challenges that require problem solvers with the energy to persist.

Many academics are very confused about the relationship between time and money, and for good reason. Labor in the academy is valued and rewarded differently than it is in any other professional context. As you plan your pricing strategy, bear in mind that the discourse on the relationship between labor and money in the academy is radically different from markets outside of higher education. Take, for example, the massive

◇◇◇◇◇◇◇◇◇◇◇◇◇◇◇◇◇ **SCENARIO** ◇◇◇◇◇◇◇◇◇◇◇◇◇◇◇◇◇

# Pricing in Context: Taylor the Translator

Taylor took their first freelance gig partway through their degree in Romance languages and literatures, when a colleague in the English Department needed help translating a Colombian newspaper article for a term paper. Taylor charged their colleague $20 to complete the translation in a few hours, smack in the middle of Taylor's own chaotic term-paper-writing frenzy. When the colleague cited Taylor's translation in their paper, the professor leading the class noticed, and they reached out to Taylor to request support with their own project. After that, faculty requests started trickling, then snowballing, and Taylor started a collection of praise from scholars who continue to send their friends over. After a few more successful translations for hire, Taylor created a simple website and started posting quotes from clients as testimonials along with their academic CV and growing freelance portfolio.

Six months after graduation, Taylor has become the go-to translator for a network of literary scholars across several universities. They have discovered an emerging niche in translating medieval French, Spanish, and Latin, as no other freelancers seem to have the skill set to do that work. Still, Taylor has no idea what or how to charge them.

What should Taylor do?

◇◇◇◇◇◇◇◇◇◇◇◇◇◇◇◇◇◇◇◇◇◇◇◇◇◇◇◇◇◇◇◇◇◇◇◇◇◇◇◇◇◇◇◇◇◇◇◇◇◇◇

amount of time and intellectual labor involved in the organization of conferences and development of publications. The prestige economy within higher education trains us to devalue our currency in other contexts.

When negotiating your salary with a potential employer, it is wise to wait for them to make the first offer and to hold off on naming your terms until you have that offer in writing.[1] When negotiating with clients, on the other hand, it benefits you to craft a proposal and send it to your client for review. While clients will sometimes predetermine pricing and deliverables on the basis of their budget or the specificity of their request, they almost certainly know less than you do about what it will take to get the job done. Often, they underestimate the complexity of the work and the steps required to satisfy their expectations. To make sure you get paid fairly, you have to not only determine your rates but also be willing to ask for what you are worth.

## *Three Reasons to Charge What You're Worth*

As a business owner who works mostly with academics, I advocate daily for the value of my time, my services, and my enterprise. Listening to underfunded faculty, exploited graduate students, and the persistent hater in my own head, I have heard so many terrible arguments for underselling and undercharging. Let's give those voices a break, shall we? Here are three reasons to charge what you're worth:

### REASON 1. YOUR WORK HAS VALUE

What is your time worth to you? What is it worth to someone else? One of the most common mistakes humanist freelancers make is to accept the rate offered without negotiating for more. If you think the rate you've come up with is too high, consider first that you may be undervaluing yourself. "Impostor syndrome" is one of the few concepts that slide easily across academia and entrepreneurship with minimal translation, as both contexts require us to continuously reposition ourselves relative to murky parameters and expectations. Many freelancers struggle with charging fair rates in the early stages of their businesses, particularly when they are unaccustomed to receiving appropriate compensation for their skill

## 72  HUSTLES FOR HUMANISTS

levels. As Caterine writes, "There's no shame in wanting to receive fair compensation for your work—and thus no reason to scoff at the idea of demanding it from your employer."[2] The same is true for working with clients as a business owner.

### REASON 2. YOU CAN'T EAT PRESTIGE

Working in the academy primes us to offer our labor in exchange for vague promises of prestige and goodwill. The mystique of the faculty lifestyle suggests academic freedom and total agency over your schedule. In reality, the tenuous connection between compensation and core professional activities like publishing, department service, and mentorship makes it extremely difficult to say with certainty that any new ask is out of bounds. These labor conditions can be devastating for graduate students, who operate in continuous financial precarity and whose contributions are recognized not through a conventional salary but through a stipend that is ostensibly meant to sustain the life of the mind with room and board. Couple that precarity with a capricious job market and nebulous metrics for professional advancement, and you've got yourself a recipe for uncounted and unchecked expectations for what you can and should offer for free.

Your business cannot survive unless you find a way to cover your costs. To thrive, you need to fully appreciate how your contributions will benefit your customer. As Katie Rose Guest Pryal writes in *The Freelance Academic*, "Don't allow yourself to be exploited."[3]

### REASON 3. UNDERCHARGING HURTS US ALL

It's your prerogative to offer discounted rates or volunteer services, and you may choose to do so when you see a strategic benefit that takes a form other than cold, hard cash. Even as the founder of a for-profit business, I pay to present at a conference or two per year to test new material and make connections. I have written without compensation for media outlets like *Inside Higher Ed*, and those articles have had an immediate impact on my newsletter sign-ups and, I've learned anecdotally, gotten my name on syllabuses for the kinds of professional development courses that, I hope, will adopt this book. Resources I create, like the *Hikma Collective*

*Podcast,* are free to the public but not to me. One of my most painful lessons as a business owner is that it's critical to know, to the extent possible, which of your nonbillable activities are benefiting your business and which ones are devaluing your services.

Advocating for yourself is good for your business and for other knowledge workers in your community. Understanding when your "free" labor devalues your services is critical not only for sustaining your own business but also for participating in a community of professionals who may not have the luxury of working for free. In the words of the professional writer and speaker Rusul Alrubail, "It's important to recognize that all writers need to be compensated for their work. It's also crucial to realize that women of color often are underappreciated and underpaid for writing and sharing their knowledge."[4] When you give away your services for cheap or free, it makes it that much harder for people offering similar services to charge fair rates.

# The Profit Formula

Many humanists are used to operating with slim resources, but living on a shoestring budget is not a requirement for pursuing meaningful work. Knowing both your essential needs and your financial goals positions you to align your business strategy with your short-, medium-, and long-term goals. Building a business should be an empowering source of agency, not a new pathway to economic precarity. To be an entrepreneur is to accept a path of continuous uncertainty and ambiguity. Knowing your internal limits will help you make informed decisions about when to take risks, when to say no, and how to invest your time, energy, and money.

If you plan to make your business your sole source of income, you must consider how much money you need to make to meet your immediate needs, build financial security, and invest in the life you want to have. For full-time founders and side hustlers alike, knowing your priorities and costs is the first step to setting up your business as a system and reaching clarity to make strategic choices. Only when you know your costs and

## 74 HUSTLES FOR HUMANISTS

priorities can you make informed decisions about your business model, your target customer base, and your long-term plans. This knowledge will also help you leverage your business as a learning experience that opens you up to future professional pathways.

# Do the Math

The actual formula is simple. The execution is hard, and the mindset piece is harder still. The following exercises are intended to help you mitigate some of the uncertainty that is part and parcel to being an entrepreneur. For early-stage founders in the knowledge economy, the calculation of how much money you need to make is relatively straightforward. The formula has three key variables: profit, revenue, and cost.

$$\$ \underline{\hspace{3cm}} = \$ \underline{\hspace{3cm}} - \$ \underline{\hspace{3cm}}$$
$$\text{(PROFIT)} \qquad \text{(REVENUE)} \qquad \text{(COST)}$$

Let's define these variables:

*Profit*: Your profit is the amount of money you have left once you have collected all revenue and subtracted all expenses. Businesses that require up-front costs to get going, like tech start-ups and restaurants, can have negative profits.

If your business is your sole source of income, then your profit can be roughly understood as your self-paid salary. Setting aside complicating factors like local incorporation laws, loans, and investments, you will probably pay income tax on your profit in the same way that you may already pay income tax on a salary from an employer. A key difference here is that, while an employer often withholds your taxes from your paycheck, you as a self-employed person are responsible for setting aside the taxes you owe along the way and paying them on a regular schedule.*

---

*Disclaimer: These are some general guidelines to help you get oriented and may not capture all factors that you can and must consider for your business. Talk to a lawyer or accountant who knows your local requirements. See chapter 5 for advice on how to prepare for meetings with experts.

What is your profit goal? $_____

Add this profit goal to the formula above and keep it in mind as you work through the exercises that follow. If you plan to use your business as a side hustle to complement other income streams, your profit goal may be lower than your total desired income. You can change it later.

*Revenue*: Your revenue is the total amount of money that you collect from clients and customers.

If your business has started as a string of ad hoc freelance gigs, you already have some working information about who your first clients are likely to be and how much similar clients have already paid for your services. Later in the chapter, we'll cover ways to use this information to make initial projections about your potential future revenue. For now, jot down your best estimate of your revenue for the coming year. You will almost certainly revise this number as you clarify your offer and pricing strategy, and it will probably grow as your customer base expands.

*Cost*: Your costs include any expenses required to keep your business running. If you are a freelancer in the knowledge economy starting a side hustle out of the library or your home office, your costs may be as simple as a laptop, a website, and office supplies. As your business grows, it may come to include more complicated expenses like health insurance and payroll. To build your foundation for the long term, you must take into account all of the costs of running your business, from insurance and antivirus software to conference travel, website maintenance, and many, many other expenses. You should also factor in a reasonable amount of vacation and sick leave.

Costs vary widely by business type and location. Regardless of the stage of your business, schedule a call with a financial expert, such as a lawyer or accountant, to talk through business expenses and requirements in your region. I find it helpful to organize my expenses under three categories: operations, marketing, and human resources. Even if you are flying solo, learning, professional development, and health care are critical to running your business.

## 76 HUSTLES FOR HUMANISTS

Estimate the cost of running your business in the coming year. If you have an existing business, take the time to review last year's records and consider how the coming year might be different. Make sure to include professional development needs like books and classes as well as business equipment like your laptop and critical life needs that won't be covered by an employer. For additional guidance on estimating your costs, jump ahead to Week 11 in chapter 5. At this stage, I suggest adding an additional 20 percent to your anticipated expenses to allow for curve balls.

What will it cost to run your business over the next year? s _____

Add this number to the profit formula above. Start with an estimate if needed. You can adjust as your expenses evolve over time.

## Using the Profit Formula to Make Decisions

I find it helpful to set revenue goals based on my profit goal and to calibrate my pricing model and target customers based on those numbers. I try to revisit this formula every three months to track my progress over the course of a calendar year and to compare my performance in the current year to how my business has performed historically. While the actual numbers rarely align perfectly with my projections, the exercise gives me tangible information to determine where to cut costs and when to amp up my client outreach.

The profit formula also lets me know whether my current profit can sustain my business and give it room to grow. If not, it's time to raise my prices or test a new strategy. Alignment or misalignment between your profit and your desired income is a critical consideration as you plan the next steps for your business. Your answers to these questions can facilitate clearer conversations with your partner, your adviser, and your mentors about the steps required to advance your career in a direction that works for you. Consider them as an indicator of how much money you need to make, whom you want to work with, and what you want your business to look like in the short, medium, and long term.

◇◇◇◇◇◇◇◇◇◇◇◇ **WRITING PROMPT** ◇◇◇◇◇◇◇◇◇◇◇◇

# How Much Money Do You Want to Make?

Money is a tool that enables us to support ourselves and our people. As you decide where you want to take your business, knowing how much money you *need* to make will help you advocate for yourself and determine which risks are worth taking. Knowing how much money you *want* to make will help you think through how you want to grow. You may wish to write, sketch, or imagine what you want your life to look like before you dig into the numbers.

Start by estimating how much money you need to make in order to realize your vision for your life. The goal at this stage is to help you think in terms of tangible numbers. If you don't have concrete answers at this stage, take your best guess so that you can start thinking through your strategy in tangible terms. Then, consider diving into your financial history, researching costs, and talking through your plans with loved ones and experts to reassess your initial estimates.

First, calculate the minimum amount you need to make right now to meet your immediate needs. Consider essential expenses like rent, food, insurance, child care, and student loan payments.

What is your minimum target income? $_____

Now, think beyond survival mode to the income level that would enable you to experience sustained security and to thrive in your personal and professional life. Aspiring toward a sustainable living situation, retirement savings, and enough money to invest in yourself and your family is not a sin. "Living your best life" means participating in weekly dance classes, buying a house in the city of your choice, or something completely different.

What target income would support your vision? $_____

Many humanists are used to operating with slim resources, but living on a shoestring budget is not a requirement for pursuing meaningful work. Knowing both your essential needs and your financial goals positions you to align your business strategy with your short-, medium-, and long-term goals.

◇◇◇◇◇◇◇◇◇◇◇◇◇◇◇◇◇◇◇◇◇◇◇◇◇◇◇◇◇◇◇◇◇◇◇◇◇◇◇◇◇◇◇◇

# Situate Your Value in Context

As the internal system of your business changes, you may need to invest more in your business to deliver higher value to your clients. Hikma started with me and a laptop, and I was extremely pleased that we were "self-generating" by our second month, meaning that I was able to cover my laptop with the payment from my first invoice. In those days, I took nearly any opportunity that came through my door, partially to boost revenue, partially to build relationships, and partially to learn through many minor experiments which services I could deliver most effectively. After about six hectic months of saying yes to far too many projects, I became aware of which types of work came naturally and which engagements were more of a struggle. I started doubling down on the clients who were easier to work with, meaning that I reserved more time for them and passed up on projects that would distract my focus from their needs. Instead of twelve clients paying middling rates for twelve short-term wins, I reined my roster into five core clients whose work I found deeply inspiring. When three of these clients told me that I wasn't charging enough, I knew I needed to reexamine my approach.

I call this formula the "baseline" because you can and should adjust it over time based on a wide range of internal and external factors. Your hourly rate should account not only for the minutes and hours you spend doing billable work for the client but also for all of the peripheral costs associated with running your business. Even if you were to build a solid roster of billable client work in exactly the right sequence without any breaks, you would require additional time to build relationships with your clients, draft invoices and contracts, and take care of the many odds and ends that go into business operations. To grow your business, you may need to build tools or hire and train people, both of which require additional nonbillable time.

## *Calculate Your Baseline Rate*

If your business is service based, your hourly rate is the foundation of your pricing strategy. It is the best approximation of the nexus between the "internal" factors mentioned earlier, the costs to you of doing business, and the "external" factors that position your value relative to your market and your customer's needs. The process of setting an hourly rate will guide you to connect labor that unfolds organically to specific financial goals by providing you with a tangible indicator of whether your actual revenue matches your research and planning. For many of us coming out of the academic space, tracking hours is the administrative equivalent of having our teeth pulled. It can feel like an encroachment on our free spirits and a curb to our creativity. I, too, loathe tracking my hours, I sometimes forget, and I confess that I don't do it as rigorously as I would like to.

Instead of thinking of hours tracking as an inhibitor, an alternative mindset that may help is this: assigning a hard number to your worth can empower you to make decisions, instead of letting clients or happenstance make them for you. How long do specific jobs actually take? How are you calibrating your worth relative to others offering similar services? Are the fees you are charging now sustainable for yourself and your business? These are questions that you must answer for yourself to take agency over your business. The answers may come in handy when you come across clients whose operations require hourly billing in order to work with you and also for cases when you need to have a conversation with a client about scope creep. There are free and affordable tools available to help you with tracking and reporting your hours. For instance, I have been using free tools like MyHours and Toggl since my dissertation to track and honestly assess how much time I spend on different tasks. Allocating specific time blocks in your calendar to specific tasks can also be a powerful motivator to predict how long a task will take and then determine whether your prediction matches the reality.

Your hourly rate should reflect the fact that you can't bill for every hour in your workday. It should capture all of the costs of doing business that enable you to create value for your clients, who benefit from your services. Often, defining your hourly rate is easier said than done. Consultants have a reputation for guarding their rates like dragons guarding magical eggs in their glittery dragon caves. In my experience, the hesitation to share rates is partially a protective instinct and partially a recognition that,

## 80 HUSTLES FOR HUMANISTS

when providing services in the knowledge economy, so much of pricing is trial and error. After four years running a successful business, I feel confident that I quote my clients fairly, but I have also come to expect that an unknown curve ball will test the boundaries of my scope of work. As a baseline, your hourly rate should cover your desired income as well as the costs of running your business. Your fees must balance out those costs for your business to be viable.

As a starting point, I'll share the general formula that was offered to me by consultant friends and sources across the internet when I started my business. While the specific advice varied slightly, the gist was a calculation based on personal financial goals. For our purposes, I'll call this the *baseline rate formula*. This formula calculates your baseline rate according to two factors: revenue and the total number of hours you plan to work per year. For self-employed knowledge workers, a general rule of thumb is that, for every hour you spend delivering services to clients, you are likely to spend one or two additional hours on other tasks to operate your business. For this reason, your hourly rate should be two to three times the rate of pay you would expect from an employer, including both salary and benefits.

## *Calculate Your Hourly Rate with the Baseline Rate Formula*

$$\$ \underline{\hspace{3cm}} = [\$\underline{\hspace{3cm}} * 3] - \underline{\hspace{4cm}}$$

(BASELINE RATE)        (REVENUE)        (TOTAL WORKING HOURS PER YEAR)

Let's define these variables:

*Baseline rate*: Your baseline rate is the unit that you will use to calculate the minimum pricing you'll need to charge for a given service to meet your profit and revenue goals. In other words, it is the minimum rate you should charge for billable hours.

*Revenue*: As we saw in our breakdown of the profit formula, your revenue is the total amount of money that you collect from customers. You can use the profit formula to estimate your desired revenue by subtracting your anticipated costs from your desired profit.

*Working hours*: Many consultants estimate that only a half to a third of the time you spend running your business will be directly "billable," meaning focused on work for which clients are paying you. You will probably spend the other half or two-thirds of your time on activities such as setting up your business registration, writing proposals and contracts, invoicing, checking your inbox, networking, maintaining your web presence, learning new skills, and doing research. Reading this book, for example, is one way you are developing your business, but you are probably not getting paid to do it.

In the United States, many middle-class employees in salaried jobs work forty hours per week and anticipate at least two weeks of paid vacation and two weeks of paid sick leave per year. If this is your benchmark, then you might choose to start with 1,920 as your working hours per year (40 hours × 48 weeks). This assumes that you will pay yourself for vacation and sick leave. If your business is part-time, or if you anticipate less than forty hours in your work week, adjust your total working hours accordingly.

Note that it can take months, if not years, to attract a steady stream of clients, and you may not be able to meet your target "billable hours" right away. Also consider that early-stage business owners are likely to spend more time on nonbillable activities both because of up-front setup and because of the steep learning curve. Be honest with yourself about the total amount of time you can feasibly spend on client work per year. It takes time to secure enough client work for every hour in the workday.

# How to Price Your Services: Some Options

Honestly assessing your baseline rate is a powerful mechanism to make the best decisions for your business—that said, quoting your clients your baseline rate is probably not the pricing strategy that will serve you best. When it comes to determining what you will charge for your products or services, I encourage you to think of your internal costs as the lower bound of your pricing targets. There is a difference between knowing your baseline rate and communicating it to your clients. While it is critical to get clear on your rate for yourself, I encourage you to treat this rate as one building block in the broader architecture of every client engagement. To take this metaphor further, the proposal you make to a client is the blueprint for this engagement.

We are about to step through three of many pricing models available to you: charging by the hour, charging by the word or page, and charging by the project. These are the pricing models that I have found to be most common in humanities freelance work such as editing, indexing, tutoring, creative design, and translation. They also demonstrate some of the key considerations behind the way you set parameters and communicate your value. As you choose how to price your services, consider whether you are framing your value in terms of inputs, outputs, or outcomes. As you weigh the pricing models available to you, consider what your rates communicate to your client about how you will work together.

## Charging by the Hour

When you charge by the hour, you and your client agree in advance to a set rate that they will pay for your time. Charging by the hour means charging by inputs: your clients pay you for the time you put in rather than the results that emerge from your work. This model is most closely aligned with the conventional agreements between employers and employees, where the employee is paid to show up on a set schedule. Most clients who pay you by the hour will require you to track and report your hours.

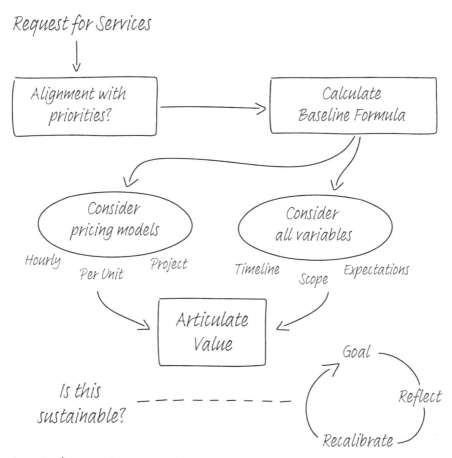

Assessing how to price your services

They will probably expect you to estimate your time commitment up front. For me, this undercuts the supposed flexibility and transparency of hourly rates.

In my own business, there are only two circumstances in which I will charge by the hour. The first is for clients with whom I have a very strong relationship, whom I enjoy working with on an ad hoc basis, and who trust me to report my hours accurately. I love the flexibility of collaborating with these clients as their work progresses and dropping into their projects for targeted advice and editing. When I take on these hourly engagements, I include a minimum number of hours per month in the contract to make sure that I hold time in my calendar and to mitigate the risk of a financial dry spell in my cash flow. If I anticipate a heavy workload, I may also add a maximum number of hours.

The second context in which I will offer hourly rates is in large-scale contracts where the client has engaged me to work on a massive, complicated project over several months or more. Sprawling projects with many collaborators have a tendency to spawn meandering meetings that clog my calendar and interrupt developmental work that requires my focus. When I join projects that have a lot of cooks in the kitchen, I have taken to adding a maximum number of "meeting hours" in my contract and articulating an hourly rate for additional meetings.

This approach enables me to have frank conversations about whether my participation in a particular meeting is a good use of my client's resources. These intermittent check-ins remind clients of the value of my time and, often, lead to conversations about where my input best serves their project. As we'll discuss in chapter 4, these intermittent check-ins build the foundations for sustainable, generative client relationships.

If you choose to charge by the hour, make sure that you are accounting for your value, your expenses, and the considerable nonbillable time you spend developing your business. I second Pryal on this one: "If you're a new freelancer, I can tell you right now that your hourly rate is too low. It just is. Go raise it."[5] Don't corner yourself into undercharging in perpetuity.

*Pros of charging by the hour*: Theoretically, pricing by the hour enables a certain level of transparency and takes some of the guesswork out of project planning. It can enable potential clients to compare "apples to apples," streamlining their decision-making and reporting processes. Some customers will only pay by the hour, and that structure may eliminate the risk of committing to a scope of work that takes more time than you thought it would.

*Cons of charging by the hour*: On the other hand, unless your agreement states otherwise, those same customers may give you less work than you had anticipated, making it harder for you to predict when and how much you will get paid. Charging by the hour also makes it more difficult to raise your rates—once the cat is out of the bag, clients may pass along your rate to potential new clients. What do you say when someone you want to work with asks you why you charged their colleague 50 percent less?

### TIPS FOR NEGOTIATING YOUR HOURLY RATE

- Specify a minimum and maximum number of hours.
- Clarify the frequency and detail of reporting you will need to provide.
- Charge extra for late cancellations and rush orders.

## Charging by the Word or Page

Charging by units such as the word or page is common in many fields popular among humanists, such as editing, indexing, and translating. In some cases, professional associations or publishers have created set rubrics indicating a set price or range to charge per unit. For example, the Editorial Freelancers Association provides a grid of recommended rates for various editorial services, and the Literary Translators' Association of Canada indicates specific per word and event sponsorship rates.[6] Both organizations clarify that rates can vary widely and should be negotiated on a case-by-case basis. When you charge by the word or page, you are charging for outputs, meaning the tangible units that the client will receive.

*Pros of charging by the unit*: If you are efficient with your time, charging by the word, page, or similar unit can mean a higher hourly rate. In some cases, you can use existing rubrics to bolster your argument for your pricing, and having a set process for yourself may make it easier for you to price relatively straightforward services. Many clients will appreciate knowing up front exactly what the job will cost.

*Cons of charging by the unit*: The drawback of standardized pricing is that you have less control over raising your rates. If there are advertised standards, you may need to work harder to differentiate yourself from other providers who charge less. Per-unit services are rarely as "apples to apples" as they may seem on the outside—an editor with specialized expertise in the field or format, for example, will probably offer more tailored services than an editor with less relevant expertise.

It can be difficult and confusing to your clients to charge different hourly rates for different types of services that you offer in the same contract, such as specialized narrative review versus a simple copyedit of a research document. Consider the unique value that you offer to your clients, and make sure to articulate that value both in the way that you position your expertise and in the way that you design your offerings.

## TIPS FOR NEGOTIATING YOUR WORD OR PAGE RATE

- Research market standards to educate yourself about what similar providers charge.

- Advocate for the value of your unique expertise and differentiate your services from others.

- Charge extra for rush orders, additional revisions, and specialized services.

## *Charging by the Project*

In chapter 2, you broke down the services you'd like to offer into three possible scopes of work. Charging for a scope of deliverables is often called "project rate," "productizing," "fixed cost," and, my personal favorite, "value-based pricing." While business experts might push back on the subtle differences between those approaches, the core idea is that this mode of pricing charges for outcomes rather than units or time. Outcomes are similar to outputs but often are less tangible and more strategic. There is a subtle shift in focus from what you will deliver to how the composition of services you are offering will meaningfully support your client's interests.

Imagine that Taylor the Translator is working with a faculty member who is submitting a paper to a peer-reviewed journal. Taylor could frame their proposal for the outcome, "I will translate this six-hundred-word passage from French to English." Alternatively, they could add some strategic framing with a proposal for the project: "I will produce a publication-ready translation and talk you though interpretive choices that may strengthen key dimensions of your argument." Which rhetorical approach speaks more directly to the client's immediate priorities? If you put yourself in the client's shoes, which one sounds more valuable?

Value-based pricing is ideal for contracts where you are applying your expertise to help a client create or solve something specific. For example, in my grant-development work at Hikma, this often means designing a scope of work that addresses my clients' long-term funding goals. I contextualize how particular deliverables, such as proposal drafts and reviews, will support immediate applications as well as long-term strategies. This approach to pricing lends itself well to storytelling, since it gives you the opportunity to situate your proposed services in your client's working environment and explain why and how they are likely to help your client achieve the results they are looking for. An early conversation with your client and compelling cover letter in your proposal can help make that case.

Framing your rates in terms of value rather than time is a double-edged sword. The downside of charging for a defined set of deliverables, framed as a "project" or "product," is that you have to guess how long the project will take and what it will cost you to deliver what you promise. First, you need to make sure that your hourly rate factors in all of your business costs, including things like insurance, equipment, and other expenses covered earlier. Second, you need to anticipate with as much confidence as possible how many hours the project will take. If you miss the mark, you'll pay with your time.

The upside of value-based pricing is that you can craft projects and processes with more agency. When you lay out your scope, you can clarify exactly what you will and will not do for your client. You can draw those lines when charging by the hour, too, but I find that it's more challenging to say no when your client requests something time sensitive, less interesting, or more complicated than what you originally offered. Time is time, so why would a developmental edit cost more than a copyedit?

## 88 HUSTLES FOR HUMANISTS

Why can't you create that resource library that you have zero interest in building? When you define your scope up front with specific deliverables, you can answer these questions in a sentence: "That service is beyond my scope." Better yet, if you want to do the extra work, you can say, "I would be happy to do that for you. Here's what it costs."

If this approach sounds appealing, revisit the tiered scope you designed in chapter 2. Try determining a price point for each of your three possible scopes. It's easier to estimate how long your simplest service will take, so start there and build gradually. The most straightforward way to calculate your project rate is to multiply your hourly rate by the number of hours you expect the project to take. From there, you can raise the price to account for rush fees, travel, or other additional considerations specific to that project.

As you gain more confidence in pricing by the project rather than by the hour, it will become easier to define your scope, gauge what to charge, and understand the value that you offer to your clients. The nice thing about pricing in this way is that you don't have to yoke your work to your time. The "value" part of value-based pricing comes from understanding the many ways that your work benefits your clients and charging for those benefits. You create value for your clients when you save them time, relieve their anxiety, solve their problems, and help them achieve their goals. When I help a client win a multimillion-dollar grant, the quality of the drafts and other deliverables I provide for them matters far more than the hours I have logged.

*Pros of charging project rates*: You have more control over your process, and you don't have to yoke your services to your time. When you frame your conversation with your client around value, you can often charge more for less time.

*Cons of charging project rates*: It takes most people a lot of practice and reflection to determine in advance how long a project will take. The uncertainty can be stressful, and the learning curve is steep. If you miscalculate up front, you may end up spending way more time than you bargained for.

### TIPS FOR NEGOTIATING YOUR PROJECT RATE

- Offer multiple project rates that lay out simpler and more complex scopes of work.

- Factor in not only the services you will offer but also the timeline and communication plans.

- Set a payment schedule that enables you to bill for a segment of your work early in the process.

## Give Yourself Room to Grow

Let's imagine that, after researching market rates for translation on the internet, Taylor found that the standard rate for Spanish translation is between $0.10 and $0.18 per word, with $50 as the recommended minimum fee per job.[7] Taylor took a leap and went for the 0.18-per-word rate. They have earned $5,500 over the past year for, Taylor guesses, around one hundred hours of translation time.

Lately, Taylor has been burning out. The translation has been a mostly rewarding side hustle as they have continued their job search. More than eighty applications have yielded three interviews. Meanwhile, clients have started asking for additional services like editing, transcribing archival materials, and even meeting to talk through the finer points of their scholarly arguments. Taylor loves the new projects, most of the time. They are challenging and rewarding and more aligned with Taylor's own professional interests than most of the jobs they've applied for. At the same time, Taylor has no idea what to charge or what to do when clients ask for second rounds of edits, meetings run over, and they get more requests than they can handle during conference season.

Let's consider how they might experiment with various pricing structures covered earlier. Like many humanists, Taylor's business started with ad hoc requests from within their network. Excellent services led to new opportunities, extending Taylor's range and network. Despite this apparent progress, the unpredictable flow of projects and financial strain are taking a toll. At the same time, Taylor's growing list of satisfied clients is

## 90 HUSTLES FOR HUMANISTS

leading to valuable academic connections and insights into the publication process—building new skills relevant to higher ed and even helping Taylor pick up a few requests directly from publishers.

Friends beyond their academic network are starting to share translation ideas and opportunities in other sectors. A friend from their frisbee team recently mentioned that there may be opportunities in the Canadian policy space, where there is a shortage of French translators. Taylor would like to be making more money, but they don't have any experience in the policy space. Taylor asks their frisbee friend for an informational interview over coffee, where they indicate that there may be funding for this work but also mention that a more relevant portfolio would be helpful. The friend offers to make connections when Taylor has a few samples to share. Taylor reaches out to previous clients for testimonials and permission to share work samples, creates a simple website, and passes the link along to their friends, who agrees to make some introductions.

Taylor decides to test the waters by applying multiple pricing strategies to different projects. For the growing base of academic clients who understand Taylor's expertise, Taylor begins to write proposals with project rates for more comprehensive services. Rather than charging by the word, they start proposing services that include more of the elements they have increasingly been providing: meetings to talk through the writer's analysis of the original text, research into relevant references in other languages, and detailed reviews of clients' work prior to its submission for publication. This shift enables Taylor to set project rates that lead to higher and more predictable revenue.

Meanwhile, Taylor continues to charge by the word for more straightforward translation work in other sectors. They make connections with clients at local government and nonprofit organizations seeking translators for community-facing documents. Taylor cites industry standard rates for these projects, which makes it easier for their new clients to seek approval for the services from boards and supervisors. As the clients come to recognize the excellent quality of Taylor's work, Taylor develops a more versatile portfolio of translation in different spaces, a much bigger market of potential clients, and a steady stream of work that isn't tied to the seasons of academic life. As Taylor plants roots in multiple sectors, they learn more and more about the professional trajectories available to them.

# Price for Your Values and Priorities

Effective pricing requires a combination of strategies including research, storytelling, and, at the core, a clear understanding of how the thing that you are offering will benefit your customer. As I write this chapter, I want to tell you to start with tiered scopes and value-based pricing, test your hourly rate in controlled settings, and work your way up to more complicated and expansive pricing models as you grow your client base. That's because this is what has worked for my business—your experience and goals as you craft your business may be totally different. Also, given how much I have learned through the crash course of entrepreneurship while writing this book, I will probably have a litany of things I wish I had written by the time it hits the shelves. My point is, there is no universal pricing model that works best for every business, and you get to decide how you want to charge.

As you grow your business, you can mix and match different pricing structures. I've offered a few of the most common ones for humanists in this chapter, but there are many more options available to you. If you cultivate a solid base of clients that you want to work with in the long term, you may choose to set up a retainer and charge them the same amount month by month. If you build a training program, you'll need to consider factors like preparation versus delivery time, licensing your materials, and who is buying. If you are invited to give a keynote at a conference, the organizer's offer may range from zero to many thousands of dollars. It will be up to you to determine how much the speaker fee and social proof are worth to you.

You may find that different pricing models are more or less compelling to different clients. For example, clients at government organizations may be used to paying contractors by the hour or output. When bureaucracy comes into play, there can be strategic benefits to modeling the proposal genre that is most familiar to your client in order to get the contract approved. In the case of faculty, I find that charging by the project creates more value and a better experience than charging by the hour or output. Academics rarely think about their own work in terms of time, and that can make it difficult for them to reasonably predict what can be achieved in an hour. On the other hand, if your client needs a quick edit or design that they can articulate very clearly up front, charging by the output can make for a smooth and straightforward job.

Design your pricing to support the way you want to work and the clients you want to work with. You have control over what to charge, but here's my closing plea to you: think long and hard before you undercharge a client because you believe that they can't afford you. If, for example, you want to support a small nonprofit because you admire their work, that's great. Figure out how you can create the most value for them within their budget constraints. That might mean offering the most basic option you designed in chapter 2 rather than your premium service. Sometimes clients with limited budgets need to see what you can do before they commit to a comprehensive scope of work.

Once a reasonable client understands the value of your services, they will hustle to find the budget to pay you. They will recognize the cost of hiring you as an investment in their own success. At the very least, that client will be open to more flexible support options and will follow up with you when they find the resources to pay you more. On the flip side, clients who try to guilt-trip you into driving down your rates are often the most difficult to work with and the least likely to come back. We'll talk more about choosing and working with clients in chapter 4.

# 4

# Connect with Your Clients

## 94 HUSTLES FOR HUMANISTS

Chapter 3 framed pricing as a conversation that you have with your client about the value of your services. You quantified the worth of your contributions not only in terms of what it costs to run your business but also as a reflection of the change you create for those who benefit from your work. In this chapter, we step through how to initiate, maintain, and deepen that conversation with empathy, curiosity, and clear communication. Through the lessons and exercises provided, you will learn to:

- Set clear expectations with clients

- Write better emails

- Drive your sales process

- Manage projects as they grow

# Why Client Relationships Matter

Getting my first invoice paid was a slog. My client was a faculty member whose institution had recently turned over its provider management system, meaning that the finance office was encountering all kinds of mysterious glitches. I was a new business owner just learning the ropes, and I was spending hours bouncing from office to office to get the invoice paid. This client was there to back me up, copying me on emails to staff members at multiple decision-making levels to make sure that her bill got paid on time. I learned through that process how to craft an invoice that would sail through, which magic words to use with administrators, and which levers to pull to advocate for myself in complex bureaucratic systems. I also learned that relationships shape every dimension of business development.

All the marketing in the world won't outweigh a solid referral from a client who thinks the world of you. Clients who come back to you and refer others bring not only increased revenue but also feedback and opportunities that may not have been on your radar. When you establish trust with clients and frame the relationship as a collaboration to achieve shared goals, doors open. Instead of trying to guess what hypothetical clients might pay for, existing clients will tell you what they need. If conflicts arise, you will have a stronger foundation to manage them. After the contract ends, you will have pathways for future collaboration, partnership, and community. Authentic client relationships enrich the process of entrepreneurship by bringing joy and connection to the work.

Like everything else about your business, nurturing client relationships is a process that you will tailor to your unique circumstances over time. In this chapter, I offer some strategies that have helped me advance meaningful work with wonderful clients who pay me fair rates. Take what is useful, and scrap or modify the rest to suit your needs.

## Get to Know Your Client

As you drilled down into one potential service in chapter 2, you may have noticed that the nature of the service you offer is highly dependent on your target customer. A faculty member with a research budget, for example, may be disposed to pay significantly more for a copyediting job that is, in practice, equivalent in time and complexity to copyediting a master's student's thesis. Likewise, translating a brochure for a local religious organization may command a lower fee than doing the same amount of work for a major corporation. In this chapter, we'll dive deeper into how you can get to know your ideal customer, build strong client relationships, and develop your business in the direction you want to go.

While the resources and exercises provided in the previous chapters lay the groundwork for negotiation, the most critical factor to your scope and compensation is, of course, your customer. The customer base you choose to work with will be a function of a number of factors such as your revenue goals, your geographic preferences, your existing relationships, and your long-term vision for your business. If your primary goal is to maximize your revenue, you may choose to focus your efforts on building a client base with deeper pockets. If your goal is to strengthen a specific social network with shared interests, you may wish to target clients who can help you build those bridges. Both of these are valid choices, as are many other motivators that may shape your business strategy. For many of us, there are multiple factors that may influence the clients you pursue in the earliest stages of your business. The critical bit is to clarify your priorities and to let those priorities help you hone your services and messaging over time.

Keep in mind that your first clients don't need to be your forever clients. It makes sense in the early stages of your business to start with the connections that you already have and the environments where you are most comfortable. If you've been doing some ad hoc freelancing by request, then you have already identified at least one market where clients will pay for your services. The entrepreneurial principle of the "beachhead market" is a useful way to make the distinction between your best client for right now and the ideal client for future stages of your business. As Aulet explains in *Disciplined Entrepreneurship*, "your beachhead market is where, once you gain a dominant market share, you will have the strength to attack adjacent markets with different offerings, building a larger company with each new following."[1] Setting aside the military flavor of Aulet's definition, the key takeaway is that your total potential market is so much more abundant and diverse than the one with which you are currently connected.

Your potential market is likely to grow in proportion to the referrals you get from happy clients and the width of the net you cast in seeking out new clientele. In my experience, the best insights about where and how to grow will come from people who trust you and know your work well enough to make meaningful introductions. You will need to gauge for yourself whether you want to stick with your beachhead market or explore new market segments. For example, if you find that all of your current clients have tight budgets, you may want to explore new market segments where clients will both value your premium services and be able to pay for them. In that case, you'll need to consider how to make new connections, which clients in that market are most aligned with your goals, and where you might need to adapt your approach for the context. You can absolutely serve multiple market segments at once, but do it incrementally to avoid spreading yourself too thin.

# Communicate with Confidence

A wise friend of mine and the cofounder of Carex and Anura Connect, Bill Neill, gave me this advice when I started my business: "You really want to delight your first client." He was right—my early clients were so happy with my work that they were patient with my growing pains as a new business owner, flexible when they were able to be, and enthusiastic about working together again and again. In community engagement circles, this advice often comes through in the well-known mantra, "underpromise, overdeliver." It is much easier to exceed your client's expectations when those expectations are clear and transparent at the outset. Some of that transparency comes from the approaches to pricing and scoping work that we discussed in chapter 3. There are other expectations, however, that begin with your very first interaction and evolve through tacit assumptions and commitments throughout your working relationships.

In the early stages of your business, it is likely that many of your early clients will come to you from within your own network or as referrals from your clients, colleagues, and other personal connections. In my experience, those referrals are the strongest catalysts for business and the moments to understand how your value is perceived, what you can offer, and how you want to operate. If you treat every interaction with a potential client as an opportunity to sharpen your communication skills and spark a relationship, you will plant seeds for both immediate work and long-term opportunities. Remember to approach communication from a place of empathy, curiosity, and confidence.

## *Write Better Emails*

When I was in graduate school, I logged into my email every day or two, mostly to check in with my writing accountability group and make sure that I hadn't missed anything significant. When I occasionally received feedback or questions from my dissertation committee, I would respond in thoughtful five-paragraph essays laden with citations, attachments, and sentences bloated with extra clauses. Once I filtered for newsletter

## 98 HUSTLES FOR HUMANISTS

subscriptions and event notifications, I would expect a handful of emails per week that required a reply.

As I write this chapter, my inbox sits at 2,889 unread emails, many of which are long overdue for substantial responses and actions. I do not recommend letting your inbox career off the rails as mine has, but I share this number to make the point that many of your professional pathways will probably require much more email communication than is typically expected of graduate students. Expectations related to digital correspondence can vary widely across organizations, from writing only during business hours to the use of first names and emoji. When emailing people across professional contexts, err on the side of courtesy, brevity, and clarity.

Consider the two approaches to email communication that follow. In this scenario, let's imagine that the author, a graduate student, has recently attended a talk given by the recipient, the executive director of a not-for-profit organization.

◇◇◇◇◇◇◇◇◇◇◇◇◇◇◇◇◇◇◇◇◇◇◇◇◇◇◇◇◇◇◇◇◇◇◇◇◇◇◇◇◇◇◇◇◇◇◇◇

# Email A: Don't Do This

Subject: (none)

Dear Dr. Jones,

I am a PhD candidate in philosophy. My dissertation is about the metatextual significance of cosmological references in Neoplatonic philosophical discourses of the eleventh century. My second chapter explores the relationship between precipitation, biological growth, and epistemological framing in post-Boethian cosmological texts.

Given the lack of tenure-track opportunities in the academy, I am seeking other ways to apply my skill set. Editing is an area that I am interested in pursuing. I am writing to ask whether you would be interested in having me edit your work.

I am sure you are very busy. Apologies if this message has taken up your time.

Sincerely,
Alex Marks

# Email B: Do This

Subject: editing query following Climate Solutions Forum

Dear Dr. Jones,

Thank you for your talk at the Climate Solutions Forum. I was very interested to hear about the Seattle Sapling Society's new outreach initiatives related to deforestation. Would you be open to a conversation about your editorial needs for these projects?

As a PhD candidate in philosophy with a focus on perceptions of the natural world, I have a deep interest in environmental justice as well as five years of experience writing and editing journal articles, lay summaries, and digital content. I would be excited to support your work through the development of marketing materials, reports, or related content.

With thanks and best wishes,
Alex Marks

As you read Email A and Email B, try to put yourself in the shoes of Dr. Jones. Executive directors of organizations like this one make many decisions a day, with limited time to check their inboxes and many priorities to balance. Which of the emails makes it easier for Dr. Jones to respond at all, let alone to say yes?

Use the following guidelines to craft compelling emails, even when your knowledge of the recipient's context is limited. These tips apply in a wide range of professional settings and can be used for client emails as well as informational interview requests.

### ASK FOR WHAT YOU WANT

Are you looking for an exploratory conversation? A referral to a connection? A contract on the spot? Consider the result that you hope to achieve through this specific interaction and make an explicit request.

### START WITH THE HEADLINE

Make it easy for readers to respond to you by identifying the result that you want in the subject line and by the second sentence of the message. Frame your direct request as a question so that your recipient knows what they are meant to be answering.

### DO SOME HOMEWORK—BUT NOT TOO MUCH

There is only so much you can learn in advance about an individual or an organization. There is also only so much you need to know to write a short, compelling email. Once you get the hang of it, you can learn enough in ten minutes about your potential client's role and organization to write a thoughtful, targeted email.

### PROVIDE ONLY ESSENTIAL CONTEXT

Give your reader just enough context for them to make the decision to write back. Typically, this means a brief introduction to build your credibility and a sentence or two explaining where you see the point of connection between your and your reader's interests.

### KEEP IT BRIEF

Humanists' love of context and language is a blessing and a curse in the world of email communication. Try to keep your emails to a maximum of one hundred words and ideally less. Longer than that, and even readers with the best intentions may set your email aside until they can dedicate time to read and respond.

### BE RESPONSIVE

Expectations around email response times can vary widely from organization to organization. At the beginning of a professional relationship, I recommend responding to messages within two business days. Follow up on action items when you say you will, and don't sacrifice a promising opportunity because you are fixated on drafting the perfect reply. The most compelling email in the world is useless in your drafts folder.

### SAY "THANKS," NOT "SORRY"

Only apologize for genuine mistakes and transgressions—not for taking up space. For example, writing a thoughtful email to offer something of value is not an imposition. If the recipient responds that they are not interested, thank them for considering and move on.

### WRITE FROM A PLACE OF MUTUAL RESPECT

Communicate with all professional contacts as colleagues, regardless of where you perceive hierarchies. Write with the assumption that your time and ideas are equally valuable. Even if you don't want to pursue a project or client relationship, always close the conversation politely.

### YOUR TURN

Draft an email to a potential client requesting a meeting to explore potential opportunities. The recipient might be someone you already know or a hypothetical dream client.

# Drive the Process

## *Offer the Free Consult*

When I connect with a potential client, my first step is always to offer a thirty-minute virtual conversation at no charge. If you hope to grow your business, raise your rates, and discover new services that you might offer, my best advice is that you meet with every new client before you sign them. This initial conversation sets the tone for your future work together and gives you valuable information before you commit to the project. When clients get to know you, they are more likely to hire you again, refer their friends, and come to you when they need something different from what you have already provided.

But wait—didn't I spend chapter 3 trying to convince you that you should get paid for your labor? Many entrepreneurs don't offer the first consult because they are against dedicating any amount of time to clients for "free." It is true that not every consult will lead to a contract, and it is important to protect your time from those who would waste it. I choose to reframe this time spent as a valuable form of market research and a cost of doing business, and I count it accordingly when I determine my pricing.

In my work at Hikma, I have found that potential clients are similarly protective of their own time, and few schedule a meeting with me unless they have a genuine intention to work together. The process of executing a free consult becomes a quick litmus test for the relationship as a whole. Does the client communicate clearly? Show up on time? Demonstrate openness to questions and feedback during the conversation? If not, I have more information to decide whether I want to pursue the project and what to include in the scope of work.

Some of my entrepreneurial colleagues maintain that their services are highly standardized and, therefore, that a conversation is not required to determine the parameters. For example, if you offer a specific type of editing and charge by word or page, you may be able to pinpoint your rate on the basis of the client's draft alone. The "strictly email" approach works to an extent if your goal is to continue to deliver the same scope of services at the same price point in perpetuity. Consider the possibility that your services may not be as clear to your client as you anticipate. Initial consults are often a great opportunity to confirm whether what the client has requested is a true reflection of what they need.

If you hope to raise your prices and expand your services, conversations with clients will help you get there organically. A potential client requesting a "copyedit" may instead expect a full rewrite with many check-ins to "iterate" along the way. A potential client who is reaching out at a critical point in their project may have no idea which services would be most helpful, and that person may be receptive to ideas and approaches that would never have occurred to them. In both cases, a clarifying conversation before you send your quote enables you to set clear expectations and create the most value possible for your client.

When you meet a client face-to-face (or screen-to-screen) before either side has committed, you build a connection that sets the tone for your future work together. By asking questions and listening carefully, you learn about dimensions of the project that enable you to create immediate value and understand the client's priorities. The negotiation proceeds more as a conversation than a transaction or, worse, a competition to see which side "wins" the better deal.

Here are a few tips for a great client consult:

*Before the consult*: Communicate clearly, quickly, and respectfully. Set the parameter that the consult is time bound—I offer prospective clients thirty minutes to explore how we might work together. Spend no more than thirty minutes preparing for the meeting. Do not agree to read any materials in advance.

*During the consult*: Ask questions to understand your prospective client's professional interests as well as their most pressing needs, challenges, and opportunities. Explain the full spectrum of services you could offer, but don't discuss pricing during the call. End by letting them know exactly what will happen next.

*After the consult*: Follow up within two to three business days with a note of thanks, a quote, and an invitation for them to ask questions or identify additional support needs. Set a reasonable deadline for the client to respond to your proposal. Depending on the project timeline and my availability, I typically offer a week or two from the date that I send the quote for the prospective client to choose a pricing option.

## Set Expectations Up Front

In the start-up world, removing obstacles from your sales process is often described as "eliminating friction." Another way to frame your approach to sales is in terms of modeling the relationship that you want to have with your client for many years to come. The best way to build a strong foundation for trust, transparency, and mutual respect is to build processes that enable you to communicate to your client exactly what they can expect. This is especially important during the early steps of finalizing the contract and securing your first payment. These logistical processes often

## SCENARIO

# Steer the Process: Kaia the Client Whisperer

Chris is an associate professor in history who is way behind on their deadline for a grant application due in two weeks. The grant would fund a digital humanities project that requires collaboration with five colleagues across three departments, and the task of getting everyone on the same page has required far more time than anyone anticipated. With the added pressure of teaching and department service, the proposal itself has fallen by the wayside.

If the team can't get their materials together in the next two weeks, they will need to wait until next year to apply. Without those funds, the project will be dead in the water.

A colleague tells Chris that they know an exceptional grants crafter, Kaia, who might just be available. Chris has never worked with a consultant before, but they will try anything at this point. They email Kaia, who replies that they are available and suggests a meeting the following afternoon.

Ahead of the meeting, Chris sends Kaia 358 pages of PDFs including every book chapter and journal article they have published in the past six years. They also share a spreadsheet with two thousand rows of raw data. Chris reasons that Kaia will want access to all relevant details to develop the grant.

Kaia thanks Chris for the material, letting them know that the additional context will be helpful when they move forward with a contract. The next day, Kaia sits Chris down and asks them to explain how the proposal planning has been going, where things are getting stalled, and which steps are critical to completing the grant. Kaia then explains what will happen next: Kaia will send Chris a quote with service options to consider, Chris will indicate how the team would like to move forward, and Kaia will follow up with the contract for review and signature. Kaia also explains that Chris will be responsible for supplying key technical details, and they have a conversation about the best way to communicate and stay on the same page.

Chris breathes a sigh of relief and leaves the meeting with clear next steps and enough confidence to delegate some critical tasks to Kaia. Chris reads the quote, selects the pricing option that makes sense for their budget, and makes arrangements to complete the tasks that aren't included in Kaia's scope of work.

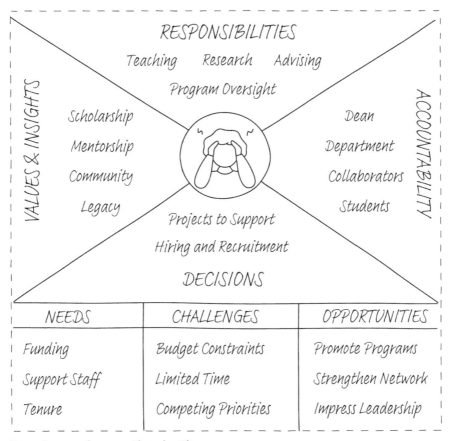

Example empathy map: Chris the Client

surface misunderstandings and organizational differences that are much easier to address before the work is under way. Clarifying your processes in advance makes it as easy as possible for the client to say yes.

As the preceding scenario shows, Chris wasn't sure what to expect—they sent Kaia way more material than needed and approached the call with a mix of hopefulness and desperation. This mindset is common among many clients—and that's okay. Few of my clients have experience working with other consultants who do the work that I do. They come to me because they want help navigating a need, challenge, or opportunity that they haven't seen before. Often, they are seeking funding and advice

HUSTLES FOR HUMANISTS

to sustain a program that has grown into a new shape. They have a problem, and they are looking to me to solve it.

Before anything is determined or signed, the greatest value that I can offer my client is to clear the path for us to move forward without introducing new stress. I do this by asking questions to understand the need, suggesting services that address that need, and explaining exactly how the client can procure those services. This guidance sets the tone for me to shepherd us through the process of delivering the services themselves.

## Four Questions to Ask Your Next Client

One of my favorite sayings from community engagement experts is this: "There is a conversation that only the people in this room can have—your task is to find it." By asking questions driven by curiosity and deep appreciation for the perspectives of others in the room, you can facilitate a dialogue in which everyone in the room can share ideas, anticipate challenges, and get clear on next steps. New collaborations with clients can raise tensions related to time, money, and power, both between you and your client and in the context of the problem they are engaging you to help them solve. As my colleague Kath Burton, a fellow humanities entrepreneur, and I have written about in the context of grants crafting, taking the time to "pause," "shape," and "make" in the early stages of project planning can sustain long-term partnerships even when immediate funding sources are uncertain.[2]

In the same way, establishing trust-based, collaborative working conditions with clients early on paves the way for future opportunities whether or not there is an immediate budget for your services. It is important to convey confidence in your own ability to support your client with the services you plan to deliver and, at the same time, to clarify that you have more to learn about the project and people involved. Once you have established that baseline, the fastest way to build common ground with potential clients is to ask thoughtful questions that show your appreciation for their perspectives and experiences. These questions are not exhaustive, nor are the answers always cut-and-dried. Getting clarity for yourself on your parameters will better prepare you to enforce them when you need to.

The secret to a great client consult is not to have the right answers but to ask the right questions. The following examples are a nonexhaustive list of conversation starters that will help you pinpoint where you can add value, map an effective process for working together, and set expectations up front.

### "WHAT DO YOU NEED?"

To solve your client's problem, you must first understand exactly what that problem is. No matter how much you think you know about your client's work and needs, their answer to this question will reveal useful information. A client who has come to you to develop the index for their book, for example, may reveal that the publisher's expectations are ambiguous or that the chapters require structural changes that may affect the organization of ideas. A client seeking grant support may explain that some components of the proposal are trickier and more time sensitive than others. Find out where your client is getting stuck so that you can propose the highest value contribution and pave the way for a smooth process.

### "WHAT HAVE YOU ALREADY TRIED?"

Before launching into your solution, always assume that your client has taken meaningful steps to address their own challenge and determined that they need additional support. Too few people in any setting are willing to admit their knowledge gaps, and voicing the limits of yours can disarm potential clients and create the foundations for ongoing dialogue and trust-building. Where many consultants might launch into a pitch for their perfect "solution" to a client's "problem," be the one who recognizes and honors your client's knowledge and experience.

### "WHAT IS YOUR TIMELINE?"

Clients in different sectors and industries can have vastly different expectations around the pace of work. These differences can affect email etiquette, turnaround times, and the amount of back and forth desired or

108 HUSTLES FOR HUMANISTS

possible to get the job done. Make sure to factor these expectations into your process and pricing.

### "WHAT IS YOUR BUDGET?"

Not every client will tell you what their budget is, but it is always worth asking. Knowing the budget will help you triangulate what you can offer that will be most valuable and feasible for them within their constraints. If a client has a much higher budget than they would need for your typical scope of work, consider offering your typical scope at your typical rate and then proposing an alternative option with additional services that would benefit them and that they may not have considered. For example, you might offer an additional round of review, additional consulting sessions, or other added benefits.

### "HERE'S WHAT I SUGGEST FOR NEXT STEPS"

Once you have asked these questions, it's time to let your client know exactly what will happen following the meeting. If the conversation is a first consult, map out the process of confirming the scope of work and finalizing the agreement. If you've been working with the client for a while, clarify what action you will take next and what will be required of your client for you to deliver what they need. Follow up after the meeting by email to restate the parameters that you have set verbally.

## Trust Yourself to Figure It Out

When I taught my first undergraduate course, many people gave me the advice that "you just have to stay one class ahead of your students." To those who are spending many thousands of dollars per semester on college tuition, this advice might sound horrifying. I have come to see it as collective acknowledgment from my peers that I had the necessary expertise to deliver valuable lessons, but I could not learn the implementation until the process was in motion. In business, as in teaching, much of the learning can only happen on the job. Humanists are especially prepared for this learning because they thrive in ambiguity and understand that every decision and interaction is rooted in its context.

◇◇◇◇◇◇◇◇◇◇◇◇ **WRITING PROMPT** ◇◇◇◇◇◇◇◇◇◇◇◇

# The Best Feedback You've Ever Gotten

Feedback comes in many forms, from student evaluations and the red pen of "Reviewer 2" to spontaneous kind words from family, friends, and strangers. Sometimes the "best" feedback is all positive, and sometimes a constructive push is just what you need to propel yourself forward. Think back on a piece of feedback you've received that mattered to you.

- What was the feedback?
- Who gave it to you? How did it feel to receive it?
- What made it the "best" (or, if you prefer, especially significant)?
- (How) has it changed you?

*Why this prompt:* Entrepreneurship is, essentially, the process of creating something that others find beneficial and figuring out how to offer it in a sustainable way. You learn whether your product or service is "beneficial" by gathering many different forms of feedback. Those insights will come in many forms and at many stages of your work with clients.

Get comfortable with accepting critiques gracefully, even when you disagree. Most successful entrepreneurs recognize feedback when it's offered, process that information, and determine next steps based on their analysis. Keep in mind that you don't need to agree with feedback to learn from it and apply that learning in your work.

## 110  HUSTLES FOR HUMANISTS

My most beneficial learning as a business owner is not that I have figured everything out—it is that I have the confidence to take on risks because I recognize my own ability to figure things out. Throughout the development of my business, relationships with clients and collaborators have enabled me to learn faster by learning in community. Clients benefit from honest conversations about what I have offered in the past and where the things they ask for will stretch my sphere of knowledge and skill set. When there is trust and clear communication, the give and take of constructive feedback is not only possible but also understood as a valuable component of the services that I deliver.

Creating this value requires a balance of confidence, creativity, and transparency. Sometimes, that means being secure enough in your strengths to acknowledge what you don't know and explain both the value and the limits of what you can offer. Throughout the development of Hikma, this approach has been generative with regard to the learning opportunities it has created and the steady stream of revenue we have secured. We attract and retain creative, purpose-driven clients who value the way that we work. For this reason, since our launch in October 2020, 90 percent of our revenue has come from repeat clients and referrals. For me, this is the highest metric of our organization's success.

Whether you plan to offer standardized services or tailored ones, strong client relationships will enable you to personalize your approach and course correct more easily when projects inevitably go awry. By investing in these relationships, you will create the conditions to reflect, adapt, and grow.

## *Lay the Groundwork for Smooth Client Onboarding*

The first consult, the quote, and the contract are all steps in your process that present useful opportunities to articulate your boundaries to your client. Here are a few common questions to consider as you plan and implement your client onboarding process:

- When, how, and how often will you communicate?

- What happens if you disagree?

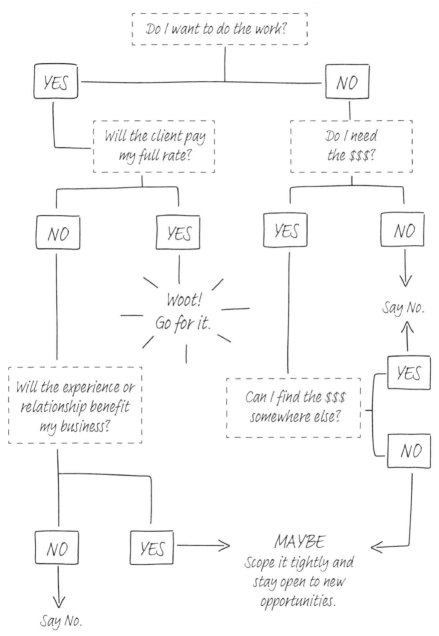

Decision tree: assessing opportunities

112 HUSTLES FOR HUMANISTS

- What happens if plans change?

- Who pays for expenses?

- When, how, and by whom will you get paid?

If you anticipate the potential challenges that the client may encounter in the buying process and take steps to ease those challenges, you have already demonstrated to your client that you can solve a problem for them. Preparing your materials and setting parameters early also signal to your client that you take your business seriously, and these steps require your client to do the same. Chapter 5 provides a "Get Paid Checklist" and guidance on how to set up your processes. The specific documents and steps required to formalize your business will depend on your field, location, and other context related to your business and your client base.

# Manage Projects as They Grow

## *Give Extras on Your Terms*

Chapter 2 invited you to draft a scope of work and discussed the risk of "scope creep," the process through which giving in to requests beyond what you have agreed to provide can push your boundaries and make it harder to charge what you're worth. Founders give in to scope creep for many reasons. Sometimes, giving an extra here or there shows a good client that you appreciate them and provides a preview of future services you could offer. Other times, we cave to requests without asking for more pay because we feel grateful for the work or insecure about whether we deserve the opportunity. We may hold ourselves accountable for poor planning on the client's part or worry that addressing the misalignment will damage the relationship.

Just as there are many reasons that founders give into scope creep, there are also many ways to navigate it with clients. In all cases, clear and respectful communication is the way to go. Clients don't always realize that their requests are out of scope. Few clients will read your contract as carefully as you do. They want their problem solved, and they will be more preoccupied with reaching a solution than with the letter of the law in your contract. No matter how carefully you scope the work and define the parameters at the outset, complex projects almost always surface ambiguities later. If you don't address scope creep, you run the risk of making less money than you otherwise could, shortchanging clients who respect your boundaries, and setting precedents that become more difficult to reverse over time.

Early in my business, a couple of my clients began requesting services that were beyond what I had anticipated when I scoped the work. As a former graduate student deeply sensitive to the norms of the academy, I struggled with saying no to faculty. I also really enjoyed the work that I was doing, and the clients made clear that they saw value in it. Should I take on the additional work? How many extras were too many extras? Would broaching the topic of scope creep ruin a client relationship that seemed mostly positive?

After a particularly stressful virtual meeting that I took from the basement of my partner's childhood home, I wandered into the living room and ran into my father-in-law, who opened a small body shop in 1985 that has grown into something of an empire in Boston. "How's it going?" he asked me.

"Not great," I said. "My clients keep asking for things beyond what we've agreed to, and I'm not sure where to draw the line." He smiled. "You always give a good client an extra," he said, "but you let them know that you are giving them an extra." When I told my partner, Omar, this story later, he told me about his first job at the body shop in his teen years. He would spend hours scrubbing down customers' vehicles, detailing the interiors and power washing the hubcaps. "We would wipe down that interior lip where the car door closes," he told me. When customers came to pick up their cars, a staff member would greet them and show off the sparkling work before handing over the keys. The shop never charged for the service, but customers remembered and often came back.

## SCENARIO

# Manage Change with Clear Communication: Frankie the Freelancer

Frankie is a postdoctoral fellow in comparative literature who can speak, read, and write in several languages. A few weeks ago, their local church asked them to translate their website from English into Spanish. Frankie saw that the church currently had three webpages on its site and estimated that translating these materials would take five hours. Frankie and the church agreed to a project rate of $500 to "translate the church's website from English into Spanish." The agreement stated that the deliverables would be due in two weeks.

The following week, the church announced that it would be leading a community-wide food drive, a holiday pageant, and an international pilgrimage. It released a shiny new website with new pages for each initiative, several videos, and a weekly blog. Frankie received an email from the church's community coordinator linking to the new site and indicating her excitement that, thanks to Frankie, the church will soon be able to share its new initiatives in Spanish as well as English.

Frankie gasped when they saw the email—suddenly, the project's original scope ballooned from five hours to at least twenty. They didn't want to risk hurting their relationship with the church, nor did they want to ask for money that might cut into the budget for community initiatives such as the church's weekly food bank. At the same time, Frankie knew there was no way they could manage the new workload without missing a publication deadline, skipping the department happy hour, and sidelining other commitments.

Frankie's mentors offered mixed messages. Their department head said that Frankie's research must come first and that they should delay the freelance work until the summer. Their parents questioned whether Frankie should be charging at all, given all the good the church was doing for the community. Frankie's roommate, another postdoc, noted that the rent was due soon and that Frankie had better figure it out.

After considering these perspectives, Frankie decided to level with their client. In their reply to the communications coordinator, Frankie expressed their enthusiasm for the church's new initiatives and the positive impact that those initiatives would have on the community. They then explained that their original quote was based on the assumption that they would be translating the materials that were visible at the time. They acknowledged the miscommunication, explained the anticipated difference in the workload, and offered to adjust the original agreement to prioritize a similar scope of materials that the church wanted to prioritize for translation. Frankie also offered to provide a new quote based on the current website.

A few hours later, the community coordinator responded that the proposed change was reasonable. As it turned out, the community coordinator had learned recently that the church was not equipped to make its website bilingual at this time. It would be far more helpful to have Frankie translate a few leaflets that were currently under development, which the church hoped to distribute the following month. Frankie agreed—the new scope would create more value for the church and enable Frankie to meet their publication deadline.

When drafting future quotes and contracts for clients, Frankie plans to define the deliverables in the scope according to the specific content to be translated, the maximum word count, and the number of revisions to be included. They will also include additional potential services, such as monthly blog posts written in both English and Spanish to update the community about new events.

The next month, Frankie volunteers at the outreach event, handing out leaflets and greeting community members. They meet a local business owner who asks about their availability to translate some materials for a marketing campaign scheduled for July. The new revenue would cover Frankie's rent for the next several months.

116  HUSTLES FOR HUMANISTS

My client and I clarified a solid plan to wrap up their proposal together, they won their grant, and we went on to do some of the most rewarding and creative work of my career. As my business has grown, I have returned to this story again and again as a way to think about how I set boundaries and how I handle it when people cross them. I've learned that you can model the relationship you want to have with your client by reinforcing your own parameters. For example, don't answer emails outside of the hours that you said you would. After the first consult, don't schedule meetings unless they are compensated. When meetings within your scope of work run overtime, call attention to the clock and wind them down. Scope creep can come from internal or external pressure to give more than what you bargained for, and it's a common challenge for knowledge workers and chronic overachievers.

Choose carefully when and how to provide "extras": products or services that go beyond what you have committed to in your contract. In my work, the extra often manifests as one more copyedit or a critical draft or a one-day turnaround when we've budgeted a week. My calculus for when to offer these additional services is loose, but it boils down to two factors: my availability to do the work and, more importantly, the respect that the client has shown for my work thus far. For clients who are easy to work with, who pay on time, and who don't require me to continuously guard my boundaries, it is a delight to overdeliver.

If and when you choose to give your client extras, make them aware of the additional value you are offering. When a meeting runs long, say something like, "We are approaching time, but I am able to stay until ten past the hour." Then, at five past the hour, say, "Before I leave, let me summarize our next steps." Exit quickly and gracefully. When a client asks for you to take a second pass at a draft you have already edited, say, "I have completed my deliverables for this draft, but I am happy to take a quick look at your intro paragraph. Would you please let me know what kind of feedback would be most useful at this stage?" Statements like these remind your client that you have preset parameters, and they also call attention to the added value that you deliver.

If you reframe scope creep as an opportunity to extend your services and articulate more clearly what you bring to the table, you can leverage new requests to showcase your worth and increase your revenue. For many of us, the key challenge here is not *knowing* our boundaries but *enforcing* them. Humanists in particular often feel pressure to offer more specifically because our work is purpose driven. This pretense perpetuates the undervaluing of creative work, qualitative work, and work that serves the public good. It burns out people who are motivated to drive positive change, and it redirects resources toward enterprises that care less.

## When to Ask for More Money

Sometimes, a quick extra that takes you a few additional minutes becomes a preview for the many other services you could provide. Even when you choose to offer extras, consider how to set yourself up for future paid work. For instance, if a client requests additional meetings to work through a specific area of their project, consider making an offer like this: "I can see that you are interested in building out this aspect of your project. Would you like to add some additional meeting hours so that we can work through it together?" If a client is asking you for advice that requires additional legwork on your part, you might say, "I can curate a list of resources to help map this out for you. Would you like for me to send you a quote?" Asking existing or potential clients about their budgets for new requests is a great way to signal the value of your services.

Many early-stage freelancers are hesitant to charge for added value, often because they assume that undercharging will keep clients coming back. I have found that the converse is often true: undercharging can mark you as a budget service and attract clients looking for a deal or an easy fix, rather than clients who are willing to invest in high-quality work. While the budget model works for some, specialized knowledge workers are more likely to benefit from building a clientele that appreciates the value of high-caliber services. At Hikma, the greatest indicator of our success is that our consulting client base is almost entirely driven by repeat clients and referrals. This continues to be the case as we raise our rates and expand into services that are new for us. I factor some buffer into my project rates to budget for this extra work up front.

I once had a client seeking specialized development of a document that required attention to technical detail as well as formatting that complied with a new set of accessibility guidelines. I let the client know that I would need to bring in an additional contractor, a recent graduate, to support the work and that we would need to plan on several check-ins to make sure that our work was on track with their expectations. "I don't want to pay for someone's learning experience," said the client. I caved and offered a rate that I knew would be too low, reasoning that my newness to the domain merited a discount. This early mistake was a question of framing: I focused on my inexperience with a particular set of targeted skills instead of my considerable expertise in researching and applying specialized knowledge.

Years later, I have come to understand that my ability to learn and adapt my services to highly specialized client needs is an asset, not a weakness. Knowing how to address client needs as they evolve is a huge benefit, and you deserve to be compensated for your flexibility, adaptability, research, and specialized skill development. In subsequent projects, my team has calculated our rates budgeting for the time to build our own capacity, whether that means leveling up our design skills, taking the time to research a foundation's funding history, or combing through policy reports to find appropriate models for the client. When we apply this learning directly to client deliverables, we provide outstanding, tailored materials that keep our clients coming back.

## When to Say No

Early on, it can feel like every opportunity thrown at you will make or break your business. You may feel internal or external pressure to take every possible job, either because you need the money or because you need the validation that your business can succeed. I received two poles of advice from other business owners on the question of whether to seize every opportunity. Some said that it was critical to generate all possible revenue and to build as many connections as possible in the early stages. Others said that specialization was key and that business owners must home in on their niche to build a reputation in their chosen area.

Ultimately, you are the only one that can draw the balance between taking on projects that you want or need and giving yourself breathing room to cultivate a business that works for you. Here are a few questions to ask yourself before deciding whether to take on a new client or project:

- How much money do I expect to make on this project?

- Am I excited to work with this client?

- How much will I need to learn to do a good job?

- Do I have time for this project?

- Does this project serve my revenue, partnership, or learning goals?

A project doesn't need to tick all these boxes to be a yes, but you should dig deeper into the negative answers and consider how to factor them into client engagements you choose to pursue. The decision tree provided earlier in this chapter offers one way to think through which projects you want to take on. One of the key benefits of working for yourself is getting to choose what you want to work on, with whom, and why. Empower yourself to determine the pathways that make most sense for your business.

# Reflect and Refine

Every conversation with an existing or potential client is an opportunity to learn where you can make the most immediate contribution. Your early projects are also an opportunity to listen to yourself. Notice not only what drives revenue but also what you enjoy and feel motivated to keep doing. Chapter 5 asks you to think deeply about the story you want to tell. It invites you to test ideas and take actions that will solidify your business strategy and position yourself for many possible futures.

# 5

# The Low-Key Launch Plan

## Let's Do This

This chapter provides a business launch plan that is yours to follow, adapt, or scrap entirely. I've broken down the steps over twelve weeks to provide some architecture that is yours to deconstruct. The steps are designed to meet you wherever you are in your entrepreneurial journey and to enable you to revisit previous exercises, iterate, and determine for yourself the pace and scope that work best for you.

# Week 1–Week 3: Reflect and Refine

### *Why We Do This*

Entrepreneurship requires you to make decisions based on limited information. You can't anticipate every opportunity that will come your way, nor can you predict every boulder that will drop in front of you. There are two things that you can know with relative certainty. The first thing you can know is what you bring to the table. Once you recognize your strengths and learn to believe that your contributions are valuable, you can go about finding out how these strengths play out in context and how that value translates into dollars.

The second truth universally acknowledged is one that philosophers have been pushing since at least the sixth century: change is the only constant. In the grand scheme of your business and your professional life, you can build resilience by welcoming the crash course you've chosen to pursue. Humanists know that learning is a gift in itself, and the cosmos is about to shower you with knowledge bombs. Reflection and getting a handle on the steps you can control will prepare you to meet the uncertainty of entrepreneurship with more confidence and perspective.

### *Why We Do It Now*

Take this opportunity to recognize your strengths and determine where your curiosity is pulling you. Revisit the exercises you've already covered in this book, and take the opportunity to decide where you want to go next.

## Week 1: Sketch Your Value Proposition

Chapter 2 stepped through how to identify, draft, and refine your value proposition. Use the following diagram and prompts to guide your drafting and reflection.

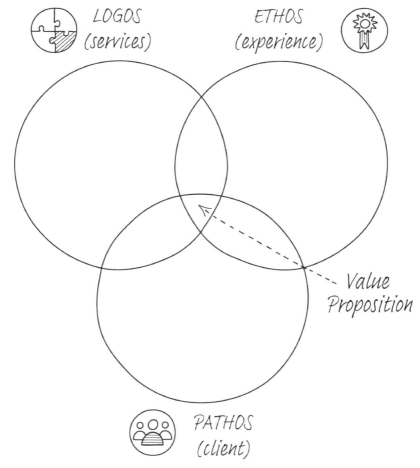

Identify your value proposition

**124** HUSTLES FOR HUMANISTS

*Logos.* What is your core service?

_____

_____

*Ethos.* What are your qualifications and experience to provide this service?

_____

_____

_____

*Pathos.* Who are your ideal clients? Name names or describe the characteristics of your target client.

_____

_____

_____

*Draft your value proposition.* Write a sentence explaining how your service will benefit your clients. Feel free to modify this formula:

I help _____ (client) do/achieve _____ (benefit) by _____ (service).

_____

_____

_____

## Week 2: Describe Your Services

Chapter 2 also talked about designing a tiered scope of work that you can use to communicate your services to interested clients. In the "Scope Options" table on the following page, start with a basic service that you can provide in eight hours or less (Option A). As you draft, jot down any additional services that you could offer on top of your core service. Build gradually on Option A to design Option B and Option C. Consider which additional services are likely to be most useful to your client.

For each option, include the following details:

- *Description of services*: What will you deliver?

- *Timeline*: When will you do it?

- *Price*: What will it cost?

- *Parameters*: What is not included? What will your client need to do or provide?

Once you and your client have agreed to the core services, you will be well positioned to move forward with more granular discussions about the terms of your contract.

## Week 3: Choose a Pricing Strategy

Chapter 3 stepped through a range of strategies that you can use to price your services. I offered a range of approaches such as charging by the hour, charging by the word or page, and value-based pricing based on project rates. This week, revisit the pros and cons of those pricing strategies and choose one to experiment with as we move forward. To give yourself numbers to work from, set provisional prices for the Options A, B, and C that you described in Week 2.

Now, refine your pricing by researching how and how much other business owners are charging for similar services. Identify five businesses that offer services similar to the ones you want to offer. Create a table with the fields shown in the "Market Map" table to keep yourself organized.

# Scope Options

| Option A: Basic | $ |
|---|---|

| Option B: Comprehensive | $$$ |
|---|---|

Includes Option A, plus . . .

| Option C: Premium | $$$$$ |
|---|---|

Includes Option B, plus . . .

## Market Map

| Business | Website | Similar services | Price |
|---|---|---|---|
|  |  |  |  |
|  |  |  |  |
|  |  |  |  |
|  |  |  |  |
|  |  |  |  |

How do competitors in your industry communicate their pricing? For example, do they charge by the hour? By the word? By the project?

Notice whether these businesses share explicit rates. When they do, how do the rates compare with your estimates for your own services? Consider how your approach might be similar or different.

# Week 4–Week 6: Craft Your Story

## *Why We Do This*

Most humanists understand the value of storytelling in a way that the corporate moguls of the world can only hope to master. In Weeks 4, 5, and 6, you will harness that knowledge to get started on your marketing and sales strategy. The story you tell about your business matters for your professional credibility and plays a large role in your ability to attract clients, communicate your value, and charge what you are worth.

## Why We Do It Now

If you have an email address or a social media account, your marketing strategy is already alive in the world. Assessing and refining the story you are already telling is the most efficient way to strengthen your credibility and let the world know you are open for business.

## Week 4: Clean Up Your Online Presence

What does your internet persona say about you? In this step, review the story you are already telling by combing the web for mentions of you. Audit your own social media accounts and any websites or blogs you run as well as mentions of you by others. Google yourself and see what the algos turn up. Then, set a Google Alert for your name to catch any future attention that comes your way.

As you get to know your online self, audit and update with the following criteria in mind:

*Professionalism*: It is probably self-evident that you should remove (or ask others to remove) anything on the internet that you find embarrassing, obscene, or otherwise undesirable to have circulating in the world. When in doubt, take it down or move it to private channels.

*Accuracy*: Correct the incorrect, and make the updates to reflect your work experience, degrees, publications, location, and current role. Check all of your links, and update as needed. If you are comfortable with sharing a professional head shot, make sure that it is recent and recognizable as you.

*Consistency*: Work your value proposition into a short, clear, and jargon-free bio. Come up with three related keywords that convey the value you want to communicate in terms your target client will understand. Then, make sure to update your keywords and bio across all of your websites and social media channels. For every social media channel you use, try to lock down consistent handles.

As you clean up your online presence, keep in mind that the story you tell today doesn't have to be the story you will tell tomorrow. By taking stock of your online persona and updating to reflect the present, you are paving the way to develop your marketing strategically as you make future decisions about where and how you want to grow.

## Week 5: Draft Something New

In chapter 2, you learned that creating a minimum viable product (MVP) can help you test an offer without biting off more than you can chew. This week, take the same approach to your marketing strategy. Choose three action items from the following list that feel accessible and manageable to you. As you take these steps, consider where you are already actively marketing and which strategies you can see yourself maintaining on a regular basis over time.

Good marketing comes from good habits, not from flashes in the pan. Four weeks of splashy content will get you through the month, but you may set yourself up for gaps in content when things get busy. Don't overcommit to a marketing strategy without knowing whether all that content creation is doing the work that you hope it will. One basic, repeatable marketing strategy that you can sustain and learn from over time will serve you better than any amount of short-term razzle-dazzle.

☐ Take a professional headshot

☐ Buy a web domain

☐ Build a single-page website

☐ Set up website analytics

☐ Brainstorm business names

☐ Sketch a logo

☐ Start collecting newsletter signups

☐ Ask for testimonials

☐ Draft a blog post

## *Week 6: Situate Your Story in Context*

Like all great literature, your story operates within a broader conversation. To find your voice and differentiate your offer, you need to think critically about your narrative framing, vocabulary, and all of the ways that your storytelling signals meaning to your target audience—in this case, your target client. This week, identify models from businesses doing similar work and figure out which genres, styles, and approaches work best for you. By understanding the norms and vocabulary of your competitive landscape, you can learn from colleagues in the field and situate your story in context.

First, revisit the five businesses that you identified in Week 3. You have already identified the services these businesses offer that are similar to yours, and you've also researched the pricing strategies and rates visible on their websites. Now we're going to dive deeper into a rhetorical analysis of how those businesses position themselves for their target audiences: their clients.

Review each website and jot down notes related to the following questions:

- *Value proposition*: Does the website offer a clear value proposition? If so, what is it?

- *Product or service*: How is the business's offer similar to or different from your own?

- *Target market*: Who is the target audience for the website? How can you tell? How is this target audience similar to or different from your own?

- *Credibility*: What strategies does the website use to establish the business's credibility? Are you convinced?

- *Content*: Notice the form and content of the website. How much text is there? How many visuals? Which rhetorical moves make the content more or less compelling?

Second, synthesize your key takeaways from your analysis of these competitors' websites. Write down your responses to the following questions:

- What are three rhetorical moves you have noticed that you can apply in your own content?
- For example, are you drawn to a particular style of writing a bio?
- Is there a website layout that would make a good model?
- What keywords would work best for your customers?

Third, return to your drafts of your bio and value proposition with fresh eyes. Make immediate revisions as you see fit, and make some notes about improvements to consider later.

# Week 7–Week 9: Discover Your Customer

## Why We Do This

You become a business owner the moment a customer pays you for a product or service. The fastest way to build relationships and learn about your business is to talk to as many potential customers as you can as early and often as possible. The immediate feedback you gather while talking to ideal clients will directly inform your research, planning, and marketing strategies so that you can set yourself up to create a sustainable business.

## Why We Do It Now

At this point in your launch plan, you've iterated on your value proposition and made your story accessible to potential clients. Now that your ideal customers can find you, you are in a strong position to develop relationships and share your intentions with your network.

## *Week 7: Identify Potential Clients*

Consider the ideal types of clients you would like to work with. Using the following table, identify clients within and beyond your network who may provide valuable insights about your market or be interested in your services. Feel free to add rows.

For at least three of those target clients, consider the following questions:

- What characteristics of this person make them my target client?

- How do I anticipate that my offer would make their life better?

- What might this person teach me about their context that I cannot learn elsewhere?

# Identify Potential Clients

| Name | Title and affiliation | Why this person? |
|------|----------------------|------------------|
|      |                      |                  |
|      |                      |                  |
|      |                      |                  |
|      |                      |                  |
|      |                      |                  |

## Week 8: Get to Know Your Client

What's on your client's mind? What are their priorities? Which of your services will interest them? Use the empathy map to help you imagine what's going on in your client's head and professional life. Revisit your assumptions and refine your responses as you get to know potential clients.

Add a "Question to Ask" column to your potential client list and identify at least one unique insight you hope to learn from each individual contact.

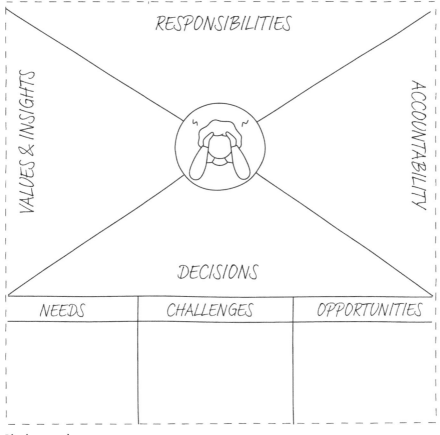

Blank empathy map

### *Week 9: Talk to Your Potential Clients*

From this week forward, plan to drink a lot of coffee (or an alternative beverage of your choice). Reach out to the people on your potential client list to request thirty-minute conversations to learn about their experiences and professional interests. Make clear when you communicate this request that you are starting a business, and explain what it is about the interviewee's experience or environment that makes you think their insights will be valuable.

Treat each interview as an opportunity to communicate your value, *but don't sell*—at least not right away. The conversations you are requesting here are customer discovery interviews. Much like informational interviews for career exploration, the objective of customer discovery interviews is to learn as much as you can about the interviewee's professional context and initiate a relationship. Opportunities may surface naturally from these conversations.

Add a "Date Contacted" column to your potential client list to track your outreach, and then jot down what you learn from every conversation. Revisit your empathy map periodically to confirm or modify your initial assumptions about your ideal client.

# Week 10–Week 12: Get Your House in Order

## *Why We Do This*

There are a lot of nuts and bolts to running a business, and many of them are specific to your geographic location, product or service type, and your unique circumstances. You may or may not need to organize health insurance or child care in order to run your business, for example. If you plan to rent office space, hire employees, or provide services that require professional certification, these dimensions of your business will require specific research and planning. No matter where you are or what kind of

# Informational Interview Checklist

*Before the Interview*

- Clean up your online presence (prepare to be Googled)
- Have a general résumé ready to send
- Keep the request brief, tailored, and specific

*During the Interview*

- Approach the conversation as a colleague
- Ask generative questions
- Don't ask for a job
- Ask whom to talk to next

*After the Interview*

- Send thanks within forty-eight hours
- Record the date, contact details, and a few notes
- Keep interviewees informed as your career progresses

*Features of a Generative Question*

- Informed by preparation
- Based in curiosity
- Responsive to context

Leverage your empathy and intellectual curiosity to make connections and discover opportunities.

While preparation paves the way for a productive interview, the best questions are often the ones that seek to dive deeper into new insights.

business you want to build, you will need to figure out the requirements and processes specific to your context.

## Why We Do It Now

If you don't already have clients, you are well on your way there. You are capable of figuring out the many moving parts of your business on the fly, and you will be fine when the time comes. By the same token, you should prepare yourself for a certain amount of chaos and "just in time" learning to address challenges that will surface no matter how much planning you do in advance. Do what you can to set up the pieces of your process that you know you will need. Your future self will thank you, and your present self will enter early client interactions with more confidence.

## Week 10: Prepare to Get Paid

The first consult, the quote, and the contract are all steps in your process that present useful opportunities to articulate your boundaries to your client. Here are a few common questions to consider as you plan and implement your client onboarding process:

- When, how, and how often will you communicate?

- What happens if you disagree?

- What happens if plans change?

- Who pays for expenses?

- When, how, and by whom will you get paid?

If you anticipate the potential challenges that the client may encounter in the buying process and take steps to ease those challenges, you have already demonstrated to your client that you can solve a problem for them. Preparing your materials and setting parameters early also signals to your client that you take your business seriously, and it requires them to do the same. The "Get Paid Checklist" provides a bare-bones list of documents

# Get Paid Checklist

| Document templates to prepare | Process components to organize |
|---|---|
| • Quote | • Professional contact information |
| • Invoice | • Business bank account |
| • Change of work order | • Business registration |
| • Service agreement | • Tax collection requirements |
| • Cash-flow spreadsheet | • Insurance requirements |

and actions that you can prepare in advance so that you are well positioned to seize opportunities quickly, efficiently, and professionally.

The specific shape of the documents and steps in the "Get Paid Checklist" will depend on your field, location, and other context related to your business and your client base. You should refine and expand this list through conversations with lawyers, accountants, other relevant experts, and your local small business support services. Business structures vary widely across countries, for example, and you should choose how to register your business in conversation with a lawyer, an accountant, and possibly other experts who understand your context very well. One of the key benefits of sorting out your templates early is that it motivates you to identify whom to connect with when you need "just in time" support down the road.

The process of building the components of your business can be intimidating, but there are many resources available to help you figure it out.

Tap into local resources: it is important that you know whom to call when challenges arise down the road. Reach out to lawyers, accountants, financial advisers, and other experts as needed to get advice specific to your business and circumstances. Seek out your local business support organization to find out which free resources are available in your area. Also consider any mentors in your midst who can provide targeted advice about your business and cheer you on in your next steps. In the first year of my business, I benefited hugely from programs offered by Small Business BC and entrepreneurship@UBC. If you are in the United States, connect with your local Small Business Administration branch for advice, resources, and networking.[1] Organizations like these may also connect you with mentors and grant opportunities.

## Week 11: Think through Your Cash Flow

Chapter 3 asked you to think in great detail about costs, revenue, and profit. We broke down the following formula:

$$\$ \underline{\hspace{3cm}} = \$ \underline{\hspace{3cm}} - \$ \underline{\hspace{3cm}}$$
$$(PROFIT) \qquad\qquad (REVENUE) \qquad\qquad (COST)$$

Take this week to revisit the guided exercises in chapter 3 and dig a little deeper into your anticipated costs, revenue, and profit. Consider applying for a credit card that you will use only for your business so that you can track your costs more easily from the very beginning.

The "Common Business Expenses" table includes a nonexhaustive list of expenses organized under those categories. Circle the expenses that are relevant to your context.

## Common Business Expenses

| Operations | Marketing | Human resources |
|---|---|---|
| Computer | Website hosting fees | Books |
| Software | Web domains | Courses |
| Office supplies | Email services | Conferences |
| Insurance | Logo design | Subcontractors |
| Professional fees | Paid ads | Payroll |
| Phone and internet | Swag | Health insurance |

# Maximize Your Time with Experts

Meetings with lawyers, accountants, financial advisers, and other business experts are only as valuable as the preparation you put into them. Meeting a banking adviser to set up a business checking account? Make sure you review the options ahead of time and bring the documents you'll need to get set up. Paying a lawyer to review your contract? Send a draft in advance and mark it up with any questions and relevant context for your business. Hiring an accountant to do your taxes? Handing them a shoebox of receipts will cost you way more than the time it takes to organize your expenses in a spreadsheet.

Here are four tips to get the most out of consultations with paid professionals:

1. *Clarify costs up front* and feel free to shop around before you commit to a meeting.
2. *Organize your paperwork* so that you can find what you need and make informed decisions.
3. *Do your research*—learn what you can in advance so that you can gather more tailored advice.
4. *Draft an agenda* with a list of questions and topics to cover during the meeting—and stick to it.

Keep an eye out for reputable organizations in your region that offer info sessions, checklists, and other resources for small businesses. If you're in the US, your local Small Business Administration (SBA) branch is a great place to start. For Canadians, organizations like Small Business BC offer regular programming and occasional promotions that make targeted advisory meetings more affordable.

140  HUSTLES FOR HUMANISTS

Estimate the cost of running your business in the coming year. If you have an existing business, take the time to review last year's records and consider how the coming year might be different. At this stage, I suggest adding an additional 20 percent to your anticipated expenses to allow for curve balls.

What will it cost to run your business over the next year? $ _____

Add this number to the profit formula in chapter 3. Start with an estimate if needed. You can adjust as your expenses evolve over time.

## Week 12: Celebrate and Flourish

Surprise! You have already launched, you stealthy minx. Your story is live, your operations are in motion, and you know what you want to offer. Revisit the preceding steps as often as you like to iterate, reflect, and expand your approach over time.

Ready for that countdown, liftoff moment? Here are some of many ways to signal to the world that you are open for business:

- Post an update on LinkedIn announcing your new venture and inviting readers to reach out.

- Create a flier about your business with your contact details and post it at your local library, community center, faculty lounge, or wherever your target customers hang out.

- Send an email to your inner circle (or your entire contact list) to let them know that you are booking clients and would welcome referrals.

Congratulate yourself on all of the steps you've already taken and decide where you want to go next. Every step is a win—don't forget to celebrate along the way.

Portrait of joy (Photo by Heidi Back)

◇◇◇◇◇◇◇◇◇◇◇◇◇◇◇ 6 ◇◇◇◇◇◇◇◇◇◇◇◇◇◇◇

# Grow Your Own Way

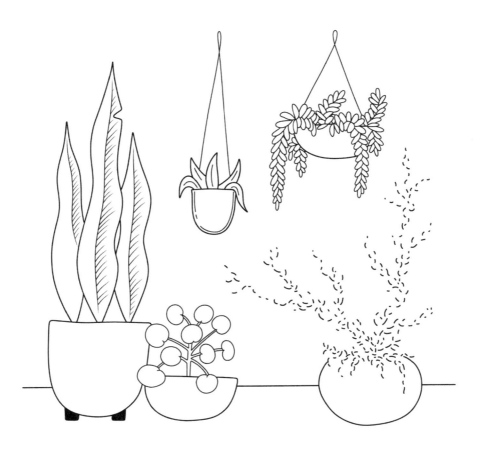

**144 HUSTLES FOR HUMANISTS**

My dad built my mom a greenhouse for her fortieth birthday. This wasn't just any greenhouse—it was a beautiful glass structure on the garage roof behind the law firm that they had created together. She could see her greenhouse from the window of her office, and she could sneak out through her private entrance to the fire escape to commune with her plants any time she wanted. Mom could easily have been a gardener in another life, and she took work breaks every day to tend her plants and enjoy the quiet.

My parents started their business together around the time my older brother, James, was born. My dad started the practice while my mom was pregnant. She joined him soon after, when it became clear that her job at a high-power, male-dominated law firm wouldn't give her the flexibility that she wanted as a parent. They made the choice to strike out on their own, in part, so that Mom could be waiting for us when we came home from school. Launching a firm together enabled them to build a life for us, and it also created pathways for them to design professional lives that aligned with their strengths and interests.

My dad is a maverick who thrives on adventure, and his unpretentious charm is a thing of beauty in the courtroom. My brothers and I grew up listening to his stories about negotiating his way to victory, leading clients to see reason, and driving opposing lawyers to distraction. One of my personal favorites is the exasperated attorney who told my dad, "I will not banter with you." (Good luck with that, friend.)

My mom, on the other hand, was more like many of my medievalist colleagues in graduate school. She was a brilliant legal researcher who nerded out on the mysteries of tax law and insurance. Many of the briefs that she and my dad wrote together made their way to the Wisconsin Supreme Court. Forty years later, I have a sharper appreciation for what it must have meant for her to take that leap into entrepreneurship just as she and my dad were starting a family. As I wrap up the final submission of this manuscript, I am feeling the kicks of my soon-to-be first child and thinking through how to design the future of Hikma around this new adventure.

The media and much of the business world present a particular image of what a successful entrepreneur has to look like. Corporate tycoons like

Elon Musk and Mark Zuckerberg are reviled and deified like rock stars for their willingness to move fast and break things in the name of "innovation" and making billions. There are things we can learn from the start-up world, many of which I have introduced and reframed in this book. Many of us need to unlearn, however, the false assumption that entrepreneurship has to mean blind focus on making money, working yourself into the ground, and sacrificing your values in the name of "disruption." Starting a business is difficult and risky. The learning curve is steep, and you can expect some long nights dealing with responsibilities that turn out to be more complicated than you anticipated. That said, you get to decide how to design your business around your priorities, and you get to define the terms of your own success.

# Learn as You Grow

Chapter 5 gave you concrete steps to get your business going, from clarifying your offer and pricing to setting up your registration and bank account. You dipped your toe into market research by learning about competitors in your market and getting started with customer interviews. As you continue to develop your business, applying a research lens to your work will help you make informed choices and figure out where to allocate your time, energy, and money. Evaluating your own progress will enable you to determine whether your business is moving you toward your personal goals, and you will be equipped to make intentional choices about what to charge, whom to work with, and when to hire people or pay for advertising. If you decide to pursue business loans, grants, or investment capital, a strong track record of concrete data will help you make your case.

## *Curate Your Personal Archive*

Unless you have a crystal ball handy, you may not know which research directions will provide useful information and which ones will lead you down rabbit holes. Sooner rather than later, it is a good idea to revisit the goals you articulated in chapter 1 and decide what kinds of quantitative and qualitative data are likely to help you measure whether you are on track to meet them. Setting up an evaluation plan and milestones is also a great way to reflect and consider over time whether those goals still resonate.

Two basic examples from my business may be helpful here. One of the first things I did when starting Hikma was to set up a spreadsheet to track client payments in one place. Every time a client signs a contract, I add their name to the spreadsheet along with the amount of the payment and the date that I need to send the invoice. I also have columns for the invoice number, the status of the invoice (scheduled, billed, or paid), a column for taxes I need to add to the invoice, and a column for notes. I have added columns over time to help track factors that support my business plan.

Capturing my revenue by date has been a constant priority for my business. I want to know how much money I can expect from my clients, and I find it helpful to compare that information from year to year and also by quarter. Since grant cycles can be quite seasonal, for example, comparing my revenue between October to December (Quarter 4) year over year tells me something different than comparing how much money I collect in the summer versus the fall. When I launched, I set a goal for myself of surpassing my previous salary within three years, and organizing my revenue, costs, and profit data made it easy to track my progress. It's also a must for my taxes.

Over time, I realized that clients were approaching me for different categories of services, and I was beginning to spread myself a little thin. I added a column to track which type of service I was providing to a given client, and then I began slicing and dicing how much revenue I was making from, for example, grant writing versus training programs. Now that I have become more diligent about tracking my hours for those projects using tools like MyHours and Toggl, I am better able to count my hours by client and by service type. This means that I can determine how closely a project maps onto the baseline rate that I anticipated up front and which of my services are yielding the highest average revenue per hour. A member of the Hikma Advisory Board recently recommended that I also start

Grow Your Own Way **147**

tracking my clients by geographic location, which has opened up new dimensions of my client recruitment strategy.

While you can't track everything, tracking a few key variables will get you into the habit of evaluating your progress and making decisions with intention. First, review your goals and choose a few factors that will help you understand whether you are on track to meet those goals. Second, identify and start using tools that will do some tracking for you so that you will have additional data at your fingertips. There are many free and affordable tools available for tracking invoices, hours, website analytics, newsletter performance, and other dimensions of your business.

To get yourself started, determine which information is most likely to be useful and which information is easiest to collect.[1] Here is some low-hanging fruit you can start harvesting right now.

## Business Operations

*Revenue, costs, and profit*: Review chapter 3 if you need a refresher on what these are and why they matter. If you want to automate your accounting, tools like QuickBooks can help you sync your revenue and expenses so that you can check your numbers at a glance and have less headaches at tax time. With or without these tools, maintain a cash-flow spreadsheet and open a specific bank account and credit card to keep your business expenses organized.

Many investors focus on revenue as a key indicator of whether there is a market for what you want to sell. That's because, in the context of tech start-ups, the goal is often to prove that a product works and has a large potential customer base, anticipating that investors who cover high costs up front will reap the rewards when the business "scales" by selling a repeatable product to a large customer base. Even if you're not planning to scale or seek investors, your revenue is a useful indicator of who your ideal customers are and whether you'll be able to sell your services in a reliable and sustainable way over time.

Tracking your profit and costs provides other information. Your profit tells you whether you are keeping enough money to sustain both yourself and your business once you subtract your costs from your revenue. The more you pay attention to your business expenses, the better positioned you will be to evaluate which costs are having a positive impact on your business and which ones are draining your resources.

*Time*: It's painful. Just do it. I suggest using tools like MyHours or Toggl that prompt you to categorize your time with standardized fields. Your future self with thank you and make better choices.

## Marketing and Sales

*Google Analytics*: Connect Google Analytics to your website as soon as you go live. You may never need most of the data, but the minimum effort up front is well worth the potential learning later.

*Communications*: Like having a dedicated bank account for your business, a designated email inbox will help you keep your boundaries clear, your business records organized, and your contact history searchable. You may at some point choose to upgrade to more sophisticated customer relationship management (CRM) platforms like HubSpot and Salesforce, which support more scientific customer segmentation and also integrate features to make other aspects of your business more efficient.

*Social media engagement*: The time and money you invest in your socials is a personal choice that varies widely depending on considerations like your target customer base, what you are selling, and your appetite for creating and sharing content. Since most platforms track your activity to some degree, locking down your named accounts and building the habit of checking traffic on a regular basis will give you insights and options down the road.

*Past and current clients*: Whether you are working with one client at a time or hundreds, make sure you have a record of whom you have worked with, what they have purchased from you, and how much they have paid (or committed to pay) you. To the best of your ability, keep tabs on how you and your clients find each other and which ones come back for seconds.

*Testimonials*: Whenever a job ends on a positive note, ask the client for a testimonial. Make sure to clarify that you will use the testimonial for marketing purposes, and provide models to make their job as recommenders easier. I like to request testimonials by email and then follow up with LinkedIn recommendation requests. That way, the recommendations are embedded on my personal profile and available for pasting onto my website or targeted proposals.

## Learn and Adapt

*Constructive feedback*: Track your clients' wins and losses so that you can celebrate with them and refine your own approach. If a client is unhappy with you, do your best to figure out why. Not every relationship will pan out, but a closing conversation to hear their perspective as graciously as you can will teach you about yourself and keep bridges from burning.

*Gut checks*: If you notice that a project has you walking on sunshine and excited to give extras, pay attention to that feeling. What is it, specifically, that is energizing you about this particular job? On the flip side, if you can't wait for a client engagement to be over, figure out why. Triangulate the factors that matter to you so that you can find ways to measure them more systematically. Once you figure out what is energizing or draining you, you can start to build strategies to create more space for work you enjoy.

## Find Your People

You may have noticed that many of my recommendations around building and tracking your business have focused on discovering your customer. Finding the customers who value your services and are willing to pay for them is a core pillar of any effective business strategy. Liking your clients, while not a strict requirement, is likely to have an impact on your day-to-day experience of work and your motivation to carry on with the less enjoyable aspects of running a business. Research shows that the cost of acquiring a new customer is at least five times higher than the cost of keeping an existing one.[2] Strong client relationships built on quality services and trust can be good for business and good for the soul. This doesn't mean that every client has to be your best friend or that you shouldn't work with clients who aren't your favorites. I have learned a lot from clients who were difficult to work with, and, sometimes, those clients have the resources to pay for premium services that enable me to make time for projects that reward me in other ways. Beyond your clients, surround yourself with mentors, colleagues, friends, and family who can support you personally and professionally.

# Bet on Yourself

It's a tricky thing to write a book called *Hustles for Humanists*. There's a lot of stigma in the humanities against words like "entrepreneurship" and "innovation," so going straight for "hustle" was a bit of gambit. I stuck with this title not only because I am a sucker for alliteration but also because it's time to interrogate the attitudes that perpetuate financial precarity in our communities. Many readers, I imagine, have benefited from the work I've done in this book to convince you that money is not an evil in itself but rather a tool that enables us to support ourselves and others.

I suspect, though, that some of you did not require such convincing. Whether you can't afford to be precious about your asceticism or simply want to make bank, this book is also for you. As we come to a close, I want to provide some language and tools for those of you who want to grow your businesses in a big way. The descriptions that follow are points of entry into several pathways for growth available to you. Basic literacy in these concepts will help you keep your options open as you move forward.

## What Does Your Business Need to Grow?

Depending on the services you offer, your business model, and the status of your bank account at the starting line, you may or may not need outside

Grow Your Own Way **151**

resources to launch your business. Different types of business, and different types of business owners, are better suited to different categories of external support.

*Bootstrapping*: In start-up speak, "bootstrapping" refers to launching and maintaining your business without outside funding support or investors. One way to do this is through "self-generation," in other words, bringing in enough revenue to cover your costs. Pulling from personal savings or household income also counts as bootstrapping.

*Grants*: You already know what grants are—what you may not know is that many government organizations, as well as some foundations and other funders, offer grants to support small businesses. One of the very nice things about grant funding is that it's usually "nondilutive," meaning that the funder doesn't receive a cut of your future business in exchange for supporting you. Just as it does in the academy, winning a grant or two in business builds your credibility in the eyes of future funders.

Grants can be very restrictive with regard to how you spend the money, and you'll need to weigh whether the admin required to apply and seek reimbursement is worth the trade-off. In the first three years of Hikma, I've been awarded tens of thousands of dollars in government subsidies to partially cover my team's salaries as well as software, tools, and research. One of the largest grants took less than thirty minutes to complete. One of the smallest took hours of required orientation meetings, iterations on my spending plan, and reimbursement hoops.

Your local small business support organizations can help you identify opportunities specific to your geographic region. Make sure to join the newsletters of promising funders so that you receive updates about new opportunities as they open up.

*Financing (bank loans)*: Bank loans are typically nondilutive, but they do charge interest. If you decide to pursue bank loans, you will almost certainly need a formal business plan as well as other documentation. Ask your bank about what is required for its loan application. In the meantime, drafting a conventional business plan is a useful exercise to integrate

## 152 HUSTLES FOR HUMANISTS

and refine much of the content that you've already developed through the exercises in this book.[3]

*Crowdsourcing*: Through platforms like Patreon, Kickstarter, and Buy Me a Coffee, you can collect donations, purchases, and membership fees from large communities of existing and potential customers. These platforms are more likely to supplement than replace the revenue you draw from delivering products or services. They can be useful not only for revenue generation but also for advertising your wares, testing market appetite, and building a following.

## *Will Your Idea Scale?*

The funding sources just described are typically nondilutive, meaning that the people or organizations that pay you do not get any ownership over your business in exchange for those payments. In the start-up world, many founders seek "dilutive" funding from investors who exchange money for various forms of ownership and control over the business. In these contexts, most investors want to know whether your idea will "scale," that is, whether the product you are creating has the potential to attract exponential revenue in a relatively short period of time. The investor may inject the funds to supercharge a not-yet-profitable idea up front if they believe that the founder and the product have strong potential to scale.[4]

Throughout this book, I've focused our attention on humanities hustles that are service based and, typically, geared toward self-generation rather than scaling. If you think you might want to build a scalable model for your business, consider joining an entrepreneurship accelerator program, sometimes called an incubator. Even without a plan to scale, I have learned so much from participating in the entrepreneurship@UBC CORE Venture Founder program. The e@UBC network continues to provide advice, community, and accountability as my business becomes more complex. For inspiration, check out incubators like Y Combinator and RevHub. See if your local university or business support organization offers a program that aligns with your goals.

## *How Do You Feel about Sharing?*

If your ambition is to grow a medium- or large-scale business, you will almost certainly need to create space for other people in your organization. That might mean hiring interns or employees, bringing in subcontractors to support larger client projects, or even partnering with a cofounder to share the load. There is a lot more to letting other people into your business than coming up with the money to pay them. I had almost no experience managing others when I started hiring, and I learned very quickly that that deficit was my biggest liability as a founder. Through lots of research, mentorship, and trial and error, bolstered by the insights of teammates and mentors, I am a better leader now than I was when I launched. When it comes to working effectively and equitably with others, there is always more to learn.

# Reimagine Your Options

Many academics struggle to separate their work as scholars from their identities as people. Entrepreneurs have a similar challenge. Launching a successful business takes a lot of grit and personal investment. It will necessarily reflect your personality and your strengths. It will require you to craft and adapt your story in ways that can muddle the personal and professional. When you care about your clients, you will celebrate their wins and suffer their losses, regardless of how these events impact your revenue. Your business might fail—and that's okay. You are more than your business.

Throughout this book, we've talked a lot about the importance of recognizing the strengths you already have before you decide what to develop next. Your values, experiences, skills, and competencies are all components of an internal system that you carry with you across contexts, personal and professional. As we progress in our professional lives, we are continuously making decisions about which parts of ourselves to let shine in any given environment. The more we can assess and articulate our capacity to bring value to new organizations and projects, the greater the breadth and depth of our potential opportunities.

For humanists, intellectual curiosity is a powerful engine for identifying, analyzing, and navigating new professional contexts. Looking at our options from within academia, we often think of nonacademic pathways in terms of buckets such as "industry," "government," or "not-for-profit." These broad strokes are useful to a point, but they can limit our thinking. In fact, these categories contain wildly diverse organizations, missions, and processes. Active research and creative reframing enable us to pick apart the nuances, clarify the problems being solved in different contexts, and identify boundless opportunities to learn and contribute.

As you move forward, carry your intellectual curiosity, creativity, and research skills into your professional development. Leverage pathways of inquiry, research, and analysis to think more creatively and expansively about the value that you can bring to new contexts. These strengths make up the scaffolding that you already have in place to professionalize yourself and clarify where you want to go next. No matter what you choose to do with your business, the practice of creating it will show you what you are capable of and how vast and vibrant your career options really are.

# Acknowledgments

The creation of this book is the best illustration I can give of what a thriving entrepreneurial community looks like. Sophia van Hees, whose WhatsApp messages with "quick pencil sketches" of image ideas still leave me in awe, also designed the Hikma logo before becoming Hikma's first Artist in Residence and, soon after, our first Creative Director. I met Crystal Marie Moten, the author of the foreword, at a Modern Language Association focus group organized by Brian DeGrazia and Paula Krebs in January 2020. Brian as well as Kath Burton, Stacy Hartman, SueJeanne Koh, Katina Rogers, Meagan Simpson, and Michael Tworek read chapters and provided feedback that has made the book more creative and responsive to the needs of readers working across career stages and contexts within and beyond the academy. Amanda Bohne, Deeptee Jain, Bill and Rachel Neill, Meagan Simpson, Victoria Sosik, Juliette Vuille, and Deborah Watt have provided sage advice, close reads, and persistent friendship throughout this process.

*Hustles for Humanists* was inspired by the hundreds of graduate students, postdoctoral fellows, faculty, and humanities practitioners whose questions about Hikma over the past few years kindled my belief that this book would be useful. I shaped the contours of its chapters through our summer 2021 Hikma Entrepreneurship for PhDs course. The course technically wrapped in July 2021, but it fostered a cohort that I consider to be the original foundation of our growing learning community, the Hikma Collective. Thank you to the American Council of Learned Societies, CIFAL Victoria, CUNY PublicsLab, the Federation of State Humanities Councils, the Harvard Mignone Center for Career Success, the Princeton GradFUTURES Forum, the United Nations Institute for Training and Research, the University of British Columbia Arts Amplifier, and the University of California–Irvine Humanities Center for opportunities

156 Acknowledgments

to workshop this book's framework and exercises with rising scholars and practitioners.

Both the Hikma Collective and this book's framework have emerged at the crossroads of entrepreneurship and public scholarship, inspired by people who work across sectors to bring ideas to life. I am grateful to Mary Chapman, Anna Gillis, Farinaz Havaei, Kathryn Kerby-Fulton, T. S. Krishnan, Shannon Leddy, Loretta Li, Lorien Nesbitt, Biz Nidjam, Susan Rabinowicz, M. V. Ramana, Rob Rohling, Charlotte Schallié, David Skinner, Wolfgang Strigel, Kendra Sullivan, Lisa Sundstrom, Jody Swift, Chris Tenove, Heidi Tworek, Zhengbo Zou, the entrepreneurship@UBC team, and so many others for sharing their stories and insights along the way. The Hikma Advisory Board members, Aaron Mitchell Finegold, Patrick Smyth, Andrea Webb, and James Van Wyck, have guided me to recognize my work, aim higher, and build a sustainable organization. I have learned so much from past and present Hikma team members, especially Ai Mizuta and Heidi Rennert, who have shepherded this book to completion and helped to dream up futures for it.

Peggy Solic, my acquisitions editor, and her colleagues at Rutgers University Press have provide steadfast support and advice throughout this project, working generously with me to create a book with an approach and a visual identity that test the limits of academic conventions. I have learned so much from her at every stage of our work together, and the book is better for it. Thanks, also, to the anonymous reviewers, for your thoughtful feedback, encouragement, and reflections on the system in which we operate.

To borrow a phrase from Chaucer, "too small are both my pen and my tongue" ("To smal is bothe my pen and eke my tonge"; MerT IV.1735) to do justice to the many other family, friends, and colleagues who have shaped me and my work. *Hustles for Humanists*, and Hikma for that matter, would not exist without Omar Swei, my reader, confidant, chef, co-parent, and deliverer of hard truths. My parents, John Machulak and Susan Robertson, created a world in which James, John, and I took for granted that we could do anything. This book is the extension of that belief.

# Notes

## 1. Choose Your Own Adventure

1. Virtual Capps Lecture with Johnetta Cole and Lonnie Bunch, National Humanities Conference, November 6, 2020, virtual.

2. Linda A. Hill, Ann Le Cam, Sunand Menon, and Emily Tedards, "Curiosity, Not Coding: 6 Skills Leaders Need in the Digital Age," HBS Working Knowledge, February 14, 2022, http://hbswk.hbs.edu/item/six-unexpected-traits-leaders-need-in-the-digital-era.

3. United Nations Department of Economic and Social Affairs, "The 17 Goals | Sustainable Development," accessed April 9, 2023, https://sdgs.un.org/goals.

4. McKinsey, "Underrepresented Start-Up Founders," June 23, 2023, https://www.mckinsey.com/featured-insights/diversity-and-inclusion/underestimated-start-up-founders-the-untapped-opportunity.

5. Alexander Kersten and Gabrielle Athanasia, "Addressing the Gender Imbalance in Venture Capital and Entrepreneurship," Center for Strategic and International Studies, October 20, 2022, https://www.csis.org/analysis/addressing-gender-imbalance-venture-capital-and-entrepreneurship.

6. Findings from "Beyond the Academy: Professional Agency and Learning in Virtual Contexts," a research partnership between the University of British Columbia and the Hikma Collective co-led by Andrea Webb, Jillianne Code, and Erica Machulak with funding from the Social Sciences and Humanities Research Council of Canada. Learn more at https://www.hikma.studio/research.

7. Loleen Berdahl and Jonathan Malloy, *Work Your Career: Get What You Want from Your Social Sciences or Humanities PhD* (Toronto: University of Toronto Press, 2018), 16.

8. Susan Elizabeth Basalla and Maggie Debelius, *"So What Are You Going to Do with That?": Finding Careers Outside Academia*, 3rd ed. (Chicago: University of Chicago Press, 2015), 7.

9. Katina L. Rogers, *Putting the Humanities PhD to Work: Thriving in and beyond the Classroom* (Durham, NC: Duke University Press, 2020), 60.

158   Notes

10. For more on this topic, see my articles in *Inside Higher Ed*: Erica Machulak, "Find Your Inner Entrepreneur," *Inside Higher Ed*, March 23, 2021, https://www.insidehighered.com/advice/2021/03/23/how-phd-work-positions-you-entrepreneurship-and-professional-success-opinion; Erica Machulak, "Professionalizing Ph.D.s by Honoring Skills They Already Have," *Inside Higher Ed*, September 17, 2020, https://www.insidehighered.com/advice/2020/09/17/importance-recognizing-and-articulating-work-experience-phds-have-already-gained.

11. Thomas S. Mullaney and Christopher Rea, *Where Research Begins: Choosing a Research Project That Matters to You (and the World)*, Chicago Guides to Writing, Editing, and Publishing (Chicago: University of Chicago Press, 2022), 6.

12. Robert Weisbuch, "Liberal Arts at Work: The Engaged PhD," in *The Reimagined PhD: Navigating 21st Century Humanities Education*, ed. Leanne M. Horinko, Jordan M. Reed, and James M. Van Wyck (New Brunswick, NJ: Rutgers University Press, 2021), 12.

13. Joel Solomon and Tyee Bridge, *The Clean Money Revolution: Reinventing Power, Purpose, and Capitalism* (Gabriola Island, BC: New Society, 2017).

14. Madeleine Shaw, *The Greater Good: Social Entrepreneurship for Everyday People Who Want to Change the World* (Los Angeles: Wonderwell, 2021), 203.

15. Plato, *Protagoras*, Internet Classics Archive, accessed February 13, 2023, http://classics.mit.edu/Plato/protagoras.html.

16. "Hustle, n." *Oxford English Dictionary* (Oxford: Oxford University Press, 2023), accessed February 10, 2023, https://www.oed.com/dictionary/hustle_n; "hustle, v." *Oxford English Dictionary* (Oxford: Oxford University Press, 2023), accessed February 10, 2023, https://www.oed.com/dictionary/hustle_v.

17. Isabella Rosario, "When the 'Hustle' Isn't Enough," *NPR*, April 3, 2020, sec. Code Switch, https://www.npr.org/sections/codeswitch/2020/04/03/826015780/when-the-hustle-isnt-enough; Lester K. Spence, *Knocking the Hustle: Against the Neoliberal Turn in Black Politics* (Goleta, CA: punctum books, 2015).

18. David Farber, *Crack: Rock Cocaine, Street Capitalism, and the Decade of Greed* (Cambridge: Cambridge University Press, 2019), 6.

19. Farber, 7.

20. Crystal Moten, *Continually Working: Black Women, Community Intellectualism, and Economic Justice in Postwar Milwaukee*, Black Lives and Liberation (Nashville, TN: Vanderbilt University Press, 2023), 79.

21. Spence, *Knocking the Hustle*, xxiv.

22. Shaw, *Greater Good*, 193.

23. Denise Duffield-Thomas, *Chill and Prosper: The New Way to Grow Your Business, Make Millions, and Change the World* (Carlsbad, CA: Hay House, 2022), 33.

24. bell hooks, *Feminist Theory: From Margin to Center*, 2nd ed., South End Press Classics 5 (Cambridge, MA: South End, 2000), 103.

25. Leonard Cassuto and James M. Van Wyck, "The PhD Adviser-Advisee Relationship Reimagined for the Twenty-First Century," in Horinko, Reed, and Van Wyck. *Reimagined PhD*, 49.

26. B Corp, "B Corp Certification Demonstrates a Company's Entire Social and Environmental Impact," accessed April 9, 2023, https://www.bcorporation .net/en-us/certification.

27. Ross Gay, *The Book of Delights: Essays* (Chapel Hill, NC: Algonquin Books, 2022), 44.

## How to Use This Book

1. ImaginePhD, "Assessments," accessed January 20, 2024, https://www .imaginephd.com/assessment.

2. Christopher L. Caterine, *Leaving Academia: A Practical Guide* (Princeton, NJ: Princeton University Press, 2020).

3. Berdahl and Malloy, *Work Your Career*, 17.

4. According to the artist's description on the card provided by @eikam ceramics.

5. On the theory, practice, and necessity of napping, see "About," *The Nap Ministry* (blog), January 5, 2018, https://thenapministry.wordpress.com/ about/; Mel Monier, "'Rest as Resistance': Black Cyberfeminism, Collective Healing and Liberation on @TheNapMinistry," *Communication, Culture and Critique* 16, no. 3 (September 1, 2023): 119–25, https://doi.org/10.1093/ccc/ tcad022.

## 2. Translate Your Strengths into Services

1. ImaginePhD is a tool developed by the Graduate Career Consortium to help PhD students and graduates clarify their values and triangulate potential career pathways to which they are well suited—you should definitely try it for yourself. Imagine PhD, home page, accessed September 3, 2023, https://www .imaginephd.com/.

2. Andrea Webb, Erica Machulak, Naomi Maldonado-Rodriguez, and Asya Savelyeva, "Moving beyond the Academy: Professional Agency and Communities of Practice in Navigating Post-PhD Careers," unpublished manuscript, 2024.

3. Machulak, "Professionalizing Ph.D.s"; Machulak, "Find Your Inner Entrepreneur."

4. Berdahl and Malloy, *Work Your Career*, 10–13.

5. Berdahl and Malloy, 10.

6. Basalla and Debelius, *"So What Are You Going to Do with That?,"* 9.

7. Caterine, *Leaving Academia*, 20.

8. Erica Machulak, "The Role of Researchers in Public Protest," *Medieval Studies Research Blog: Meet Us at the Crossroads of Everything*, September 8, 2017, https://sites.nd.edu/manuscript-studies/2017/09/08/the-role-of-researchers-in-public-protest/.

9. Arshpreet Kaur, "What Is a Minimum Viable Product (MVP)? Types, Examples, Benefits," *Insights—Web and Mobile Development Services and Solutions* (blog), November 2, 2022, https://www.netsolutions.com/insights/what-is-a-minimum-viable-product-mvp/; N. Taylor Thompson, "Building a Minimum Viable Product? You're Probably Doing It Wrong," *Harvard Business Review*, September 11, 2013, https://hbr.org/2013/09/building-a-minimum-viable-prod.

10. David J. Bland and Alexander Osterwalder, *Testing Business Ideas: A Field Guide for Rapid Experimentation* (Hoboken, NJ: Wiley, 2019), 240.

11. Bill Aulet, *Disciplined Entrepreneurship: 24 Steps to a Successful Startup* (Hoboken, NJ: Wiley, 2013), 237.

12. Rafi Mohammed, "The Good-Better-Best Approach to Pricing," *Harvard Business Review*, October 2018, https://hbr.org/2018/09/the-good-better-best-approach-to-pricing.

# 3. Name Your Price

1. See Basalla and Debelius's sage wisdom on postinterview employment negotiations. Much of the advice about constructive dialogue also applies to negotiating with clients. Basalla and Debelius, *"So What Are You Going to Do with That?,"* 139–44.

2. Caterine, *Leaving Academia*, 34.

3. Katie Rose Guest Pryal, *The Freelance Academic: Transform Your Creative Life and Career* (Chapel Hill, NC: Blue Crow Books, 2019), 125.

4. Rusul Alrubail, "Education, Writing, Entrepreneurship: Creating Impact through Communities," in *Succeeding Outside the Academy: Career Paths beyond the Humanities, Social Sciences, and STEM*, ed. Joseph Fruscione and Kelly J. Baker (Lawrence: University Press of Kansas, 2018), 144.

5. Pryal, *Freelance Academic*, 125.

6. Editorial Freelancers Association, "Editorial Rates," accessed March 15, 2024, https://www.the-efa.org/rates/; Attlc Ltac, "Rates—Literary Translators' Association of Canada," *ATTLC • LTAC* (blog), accessed March 15, 2024, https://www.attlc-ltac.org/en/rates/.

7. The Translation Company, "Translation Services Rates," December 2, 2014, https://thetranslationcompany.com/resources/5-facts-buying-translation/translation-pricing.htm.

## 4. Connect with Your Clients

1. Aulet, *Disciplined Entrepreneurship*, 43.

2. Kath Burton and Erica Machulak, "The Grant Writer's Paradox: Leveraging Public Scholarship Ideas When the Money Is Uncertain," *Journal of Electronic Publishing*, 2025.

## 5. The Low-Key Launch Plan

1. Small Business Administration, "SBA Office Locations," accessed February 19, 2023, https://www.sba.gov/about-sba/sba-locations.

## 6. Grow Your Own Way

1. What I've provided here is only the tip of the iceberg. For more rigorous evaluation methods, experiments, and inspiration, start with Bland and Osterwalder, *Testing Business Ideas*; and Paul Hague, *Market Research in Practice: An Introduction to Gaining Greater Market Insight*, 4th ed. (London: Kogan Page, 2021).

2. Amy Gallo, "The Value of Keeping the Right Customers," *Harvard Business Review*, October 29, 2014, https://hbr.org/2014/10/the-value-of-keeping-the-right-customers.

3. The Small Business Administration lays out the key components of both "traditional" and "lean" business plans and provides fictional plans. SBA,

"Write Your Business Plan," accessed March 27, 2024, https://www.sba.gov/business-guide/plan-your-business/write-your-business-plan.

4. I am only scratching the surface here. For a brief overview of venture capital fundraising in the tech start-up world, see this article by the well-known Silicon Valley incubator Y Combinator: "A Guide to Seed Fundraising," YC Startup Library, accessed March 27, 2024, https://www.ycombinator.com/library/4A-a-guide-to-seed-fundraising.

# Image Credits

With the exception of those listed below, all of the illustrations, exercises, diagrams, and other visuals in this book were designed by Sophia van Hees for Erica Machulak.

How to Use This Book: *Daruma Doll*. Photographed by Erica Machulak and edited by Sophia van Hees. Daruma doll crafted by Grace Lee of Eikcam Ceramics.

Chapter 2: *Strength*. Digital line drawing on chapter opener courtesy of Sophia van Hees, adapted from the card of the same name in the Brave Snail Designs tarot deck.

Chapter 5: *Portrait of Joy*. Photograph by Heidi Back.

# Index

*Page numbers for images and tables are in italics.*

Academia, xvi, 11, 113, 151, 154; culture of, 50; hustle, attitudes about, 16; identity in, 39; independent scholarship in, 8; job market, xiv, 2, 72, 98; labor in, 69, 71, 72, 79; mentors, 7; myths believed in, 7–9; politics in, xiii; precarity in, xvi; publishing in, 30, 38; timelines, attitudes about, 29; training in, 46, 53–54

Accounting, 22, 24, 74, 75, 137, 139, 145, 147, 148, 150. *See also* Money

Activism, x

Adaptability, 3, 61, 96, 110

Advisors: career, 24, 50; faculty, 17, 24, 38, 76; financial, 137, 139

Agency, 2, 7, 8, 26, 87; in academia, 72; in graduate school, 17; hustling, connection to, 15; professional, 17, 22, 39, 42, 73, 79

Aisle (start-up), 18

Alchemy, xiii

Alliteration, 150

Alrubail, Rusul, 73

"Alt ac," 6

Ambiguity, 3, 4, 10, 12, 42, 47, 60, 73, 107, 108, 113. *See also* Uncertainty

American Council of Learned Societies, 27

American Dream, 15

American Historical Association, 10

Anura Connect (start-up), 97

Anxiety, 2, 29, 51, 88. *See also* Stress

Apologies, 101

Arabic (language), xiv, 52

Aristotle, 47–49, *48*, 68

Asceticism, 150

Assessing opportunities, *111*

Athena, 13

Audience, ix, xiv, 18, 44, 47, 48, 130; of musicians, 15

Aulet, Bill, 57, 96

Auto detailing, 113

Bank account, 137, 139, 145, 147, 148

Banter, 144

Basalla, Susan Elizabeth, 7, 53

B Corporation Certification, 3, 18, 19

Berdahl, Loleen, 7, 27, 30, 53

Black culture, ix, 15

Black empowerment, ix, 15

Black entrepreneurship, 5

Black Excellence, ix

Black families, ix

Black feminist writing, x

#BlackGirlMagic, ix

Black history, ix

Black Lives Matter, x, 2, 18

Black women, ix

Bland, David J., 57

Blogs, 33, 52, 55, 56, 58, 64, 114, 115, 128, 129

Bootstrapping, 151

Boston, xiv, 113

Brave Snail Designs, 33

Bridge, Tyee, 12

British Columbia, 7, 18, 27

Bunch, Lonnie, 3

Bundling deliverables. *See* Project rates

Burnout, 69, 89, 117

Burton, Kath, 106

Business plan, 46, 146, 151–52, 161n. 3. *See also* Launching

Cancer, xiv

*Canterbury Tales*, xii. *See also* Medieval English Literature; Medieval studies

Capitalism, xi, 5, 6, 12, 15, 17

Carbon footprint, 11, 13, 19

**166** Index

Career competencies, 53. *See also* Skills

Carex (start-up), 97

Carnegie, Andrew, 19

Carter, Shawn (Jay-Z), 15

Cassuto, Lenny, 17

Caterine, Chris, 29, 54, 72

Center for Strategic and International Studies, 5

Change, 9, 11, 47, 94, 117, 122, 169; business, 49, 78; Lorde on, x; plans, 112, 114–15, 136, 137; positive, xvi; systems-level, 3, 17

Chicago, ix

City University of New York PublicsLab, 27

Clients, 6, 35, 40, 47, 49, 50, 54, 78, 88, 127, 133; beachhead market and, 96; boundaries with, 42, 61, 63, 79, 89, 110, 113, 116–17, 136; budgets, 71, 92, 95, 96, 104, 106, 108, 117; check-ins with, 84, 102, 118; communicating with, 35, 38, 45, 49, 58, 61, 65, 68, 76, 82, 86, 97–101, 102, 103, 110, 112–13, 114–15, 116, 125, 127, 128, 134, 136 (*see also* Communications); conflicts with, 35, 95, 103, 105, 106, 110, 136; cost to acquire new, 149–50; difficult, 92; emails (*see* Email); expectations, 58–59, 71, 83, 94, 97, 102, 103, 105, 107, 118; "extras" for, 61, 63, 88, 112–13, 116, 117, 149; first, 20, 58, 75, 96, 97; goals of, 30, 87, 88; ideal, 23, 58, 95–96, 124, 131, 132; liking, 31, 83, 149; meetings with, 101–3 (*see also* Consultations; Meetings); negotiating with, 9, 22, 40, 42, 63, 68, 69, 71, 72, 85–86, 89, 95, 103, 118, 125; new, 24, 40, 49, 101; onboarding, 62, 110–12, 136; potential, 9, 27, 35, 49, 90, 97, 101, 102–3, 119, 131, 132, 132, 133, 134; priorities, 87, 91, 103, 133; questions for, 107–8, 133; records of, 148, 149; referrals, 20, 26, 94, 96, 97, 117, 140; relationships with, 22, 31, 35, 38, 42–43, 49, 57–58, 65, 68, 78, 83, 84, 94–96, 97, 103–4, 110, 116, 150; repeat, 94, 110, 117; respect shown by, 116; responsibilities of, 59, 60, 64, 112; target, 43, 48, 48, 49, 74, 95–96, 124, 128, 130, 132, 140, 148; testimonials from, 70, 90, 129, 149; tracking, 146–47, 148, 149; trust with, 35, 83, 94, 106, 107, 110, 150

Climate, 2, 5, 14, 18, 19, 99

Code, Jillianne, 7

Coffee, 5, 33, 134

Cole, Johnetta, 3

Collaboration, xvi, 8, 19, 104, 110; with clients, 83, 84, 94–95, 106

Colonialism, 14

Communications, 8, 35, 89, 148. *See also* Clients, communicating with; Email

Community, xvi, 35, 73, 114–15; Black, ix, 15; clients and, 95, 110; empathy and, 43; employees, 25; engagement, 97, 106; entrepreneurial, 8, 12, 110, 152; Indigenous, vi; learning in, 110; organizations, 45, 55, 90, 95, 114–15; as positive force, 16; of practice, 39, 73; rural, xvi; of scholars, 8; systems of, 17–19; university, 56

Compensation. *See* Payment

Competitors: comparison with, 130–31, 145; pricing, 127; website, 131. *See also* Market research

Conferences, 17, 72, 75, 91, 138; academic, x, 3, 8, 10, 89

Consultations, 101–3, 104, 107–8, 110, 116, 136, 139; following up after, 103; free, 101–3; preparing for, 103; qualities of, 103. *See also* Clients, meetings with; Meetings

Content development, 41, 55, 59–60, 64, 129

Contracts, 2, 25, 55, 78, 92, 95, 99, 102, 110, 136, 146; client understanding of, 113; hourly rates in, 83–84; negotiating, 118, 125; scope creep and, 113; specificity in, 58; taking time to draft, 78, 81; value-based pricing in, 87. *See also* Pricing; Scope creep; Scope of work

Copyediting, 38, 55, 86, 87, 95, 102, 116

Core offer. *See* Offers, core

Costs. *See* Expenses

Cover letters, 87

COVID-19 pandemic, xvi, 2, 18, 20, 31, 41

Credibility, 31, 68, 127, 128, 130, 151

Credit card, 138, 147

Crowdsourcing, 152

Curiosity, 2, 6, 22, 69, 94, 122–23, 135; in communication, 94, 97, 106; in entrepreneurs, 6, 8, 10–11, 20, 26; in humanists, 4, 7, 10–11, 154; intellectual, 20, 22; leveraging, 16, 22; as a leadership trait, 3, 8; as a strength, 4, 10–11, 40, 42, 154; as a tool, 17, 19

Customer relationship management programs, 148

Customers. *See* Clients

Daruma Doll, 33, 34
Debelius, Maggie, 7, 53
Delight. *See* Joy
Deliverables, 52, 61, 62, 71, 86, 87, 88, 114, 115, 116, 118
DeWese, Mattie Pressley, 15
Digital humanities, 41, 56, 104
Dissertations, xiii, xiv, 6, 29, 46, 50, 53–54, 56, 79, 98; committees, 97; editing, 40, 43, 58; flexibility of writing, 31; job, compared to, 52–53; as project management, 4; skills-based description of, 52–53
Distraction, 33, 78
Diversity, 5, 12
Dragons, 79
Dream theory, medieval, xiii
Duffield-Thomas, Denise, 16

Editing, xvi, 4, 5, 10, 35, 38, 40, 43, 58, 83, 89; defining, 55; pricing, 59, 82, 85–86, 87, 92, 102; scope creep in, 41, 63, 116; scoping, *64*
Editorial Freelancers' Association, 85
Education, 5, 18; graduate, 17; higher, 69, 71
Email, 97–101; boundaries and, 116, 148; brevity in, 100; communication with clients, sole means, 102; dedicated address, 148; expectations, 98, 107; follow-ups, 108; marketing and, 128, *138*; networking and, 140; testimonials, 149. *See also* Communications
Empathy, 3, 11, 19, 22, 35, 42–43, 69, 94, 97, 133, 134; map, *105*, 133, *133*, 134
Entrepreneurship, xi, 22–23, 29, 32, 38, 39, 44, 47, 91, 144–45; accelerators, 152; agency in, 5; assumptions about, 145; community in, 8, 12, 35; compared to hustling, 16; definition of, 109; early stages, of, 35; equity gaps in, 5; feedback and, 46, 109 (*see also* Feedback); graduate school, similarities to, 43, 46, 53; humanists as, 7–8, 10–11, 18; impostor syndrome and, 71; intellectual challenges of, 6, 19–20; joy in, 19–20, 56, 95; in music culture, 15; qualities necessary, 8, 10–11, 17, 46–47, 153; reasons for, 26–27, 122; requirements of, 33, 122; as resistance against racist policies, 15; scholarly trajectory of, 24,

39–40; skepticism about, 11; stigma against, 150; storytelling in, 45; uncertainty and, 74; vocabulary of, 10–11, 38, 44, 46, 56, 62, 69, 86, 96, 103
entrepreneurship@UBC, 17–18, 138, 152
Environmental, Social & Governance (ESG) Framework, 13, 19
Epimetheus, 13
Equity, 5, 12, 18. *See also* Inequity
Ethos, 47–49, *48*, 53–54, *54*, *123*, 124
Evaluation plan, 146
Expenses, 74–76, 77, 84, 87, 112, 136, 139, 140, 147–48; annual, 140; categories of, 75; common, *138*; tracking, 147–48. *See also* Health care; Human resources; Learning, Marketing; Operations, business; Professional development

Facebook. *See* Meta
Facilitation, 4, 11, 52, *64*, 106
Family, ix, xiv, xvi, 33, 45, 76, 77, 113, 144, 150
Farber, David, 15
Fast fashion, 14
Feedback, 46, 56, 57, 58, 94, 109, 110, 131, 149; boundaries, setting, 116; dissertation, 97
Financial precarity, xvi, 12, 38, 72, 73, 150. *See also* Poverty
Flexibility, xiv, 10, 26, 39, 97, 118, 144; in graduate school, 31, 52; of hourly rates, 83
Floyd, George, 18
Food, ix, x, 77
Food and Drug Administration, 18
Freelancing, xvi, 4, 6, 9, 35, 42, 70, 114; clients, 75, 96; cost, 75; framework for, 23–24; mistakes made by, 71; motivations for, 26, 38, 40, 43; pricing, 82, 84, 117. *See also* Hustle; Side hustle
Friction, eliminating, 103
Frisbee, 90

Gardening, 144
Gay, Ross, 19
Globalization, economic, 15
Goals, xiv, 25, 33, 43, 53, 65, 73, 91, 96, 102, 119, 145–46, 147; clients', 30, 87, 88, 94–95; financial, 73, 79, 80; importance of setting, xvi, 29–31; profit, 75, 76; revenue, 76, 119

Good-Better-Best Pricing. *See* Pricing, tiered
Google, 128, *135*, 148
Google Analytics, 148
Government, 8, 14, 40, 55, 90, 91–92, 151
Graduate school, ix, xiv, 6, 24, 46; academic politics in, xiii; agency in, 17; career advising in, 50; comprehensive exams, xiii, 6, 29; economic conditions of, 38, 43, 71; email in, 97–98; intangible elements of, 39; as a job, 50; teaching in, 51, 108
Graduate students, xvi, 2, 17, 29, 39, 71, 113; dissertations of, 53; and freelance work, 38, 40, 43; labor conditions of, 38, 71, 72; priorities of, 27; teaching, 51, 108
Grants, small business, 145, 151
Grant writing, 44, 47, 58, 104, 106, 107, 116, 146
Great Resignation, 2
Greed, xi
Greek mythology, 13–14
Growth: business, 22, 35, 49, 89–90, 91, 96, 97, 101, 150; changing needs and, 68; client base, 91; "hockey-stick," 22; of opportunities, 40; personal, 2; professional, 39; projects, 94, 112–13; revenue, 75, 76, 78; by word of mouth, 42
Gut instincts, 69, 149

*Harvard Business Review*, 62
Harvard Business School, 3
Headshot, 129
Health, 12, 14
Health care, x, 11, 18, 26, 75
Health insurance, *28*, 75, *134*, *138*
Hephaestus, 13
Higher education, xvi, 6, 90, 24; administration, 8; compensation in, 11, 69, 71, 94; in the COVID-19 pandemic, 2; prestige economy in, 69–71; timelines in, 29. *See also* Academia; Graduate school; Graduate students
Hikma, 102, 110, 117; Advisory Board, 146; Entrepreneurship for PhDs course, 39; future, 117, 144; goals, evolution of, 30–31; grant development work, 87; grants, use of, 151; launch, xvi, 2, 6, 9; early days, 20, 33, 58, 78, 146; research, 7
*Hikma Collective Podcast*, 72

Hill, Linda A., 3
Hip-hop, 15
hooks, bell, 16
Hours worked, tracking and reporting, 79, 82–83, 146–47, 148
HubSpot, 148
Humanists, 5, 22, 29, 77, 117; ambiguity, comfort with, 12, 46, 47, 73, 108; definition of, 4; dissertations, 52; entrepreneurial qualities of, 10; entrepreneurship for, xi, 10–11, 16, 18, 23, 26, 38, 44; freelancing, 40, 43–44, 71, 82; knowledge, love of, 7–8, 39, 100, 122, 154; money, attitudes about, x–xi, 11–12, 16, 69, 145; myths believed by, 6, 7–9, 9–11, 11–12; skills, 9, 43, 46, 47, 108; society, service to, 8; storytelling, use of, 13; teaching, 47, 51–52 ; training, 10; world, role in, 3, 18–19.
Humanities, the: dissertations in, 52; entrepreneurship in, 22–23, 82, 106, 152; graduate school in, 46 (*see also* Graduate school); potential, 3; society, service to, 3, 8, 18–19; state of, xi; stigma against entrepreneurship in, 150; teaching in, 51–52
Human resources, 24–25, 75; expenses of, *138*
Hustle, 16, 150; accidental, 40, 42; attitudes about, 6, 14–15, 16–17; chilled, 16; client, 92; contrasted with labor, 16; definition, 14–15, 16–17, 150; differentiating, 42; examples of, 54–55; and neoliberalism, 16. *See also* Freelancing; Side hustle

Identity, 153; academic, 39
ImaginePhD, 24, 27, 39, 159n1
Impostor syndrome, 10, 23, 71
Inclusivity, 5, 19
Income, *28*, 75, 76, 77, 80; bootstrapping from, 151; business as sole source of, 4, 5, 73, 74; supplements to, 9–10, 40, 75
Independent scholar, 8
Indexing, xvi, 10, 35, 38, 40, 82, 85, 107
Indiana, xiv
Inequity, 12, 14, 18. *See also* Equity
Inkcap Consulting, 9
*Inside Higher Ed*, 50, 72
Instagram. *See* Meta
Interviews: with Hikma course participants, 39; informational, 90, 99, *134*, *135*, 145

Investors, 145, 147, 151, 152. *See also* Venture capital
Isolation, 33, 136, 137

Jackson, Curtis (50 Cent), 15
Job creation, 5, 12
Joy, 2, 4, 7, 8, 12, 16, 19–20, 22, 33, 56, 95, *141*
"Just in time," occasions, 40, 136, 137

Knowledge, xvii, 9, 22–23, 47, 49, 110; client's, 107; creation of, 7, 46; of darkness, 19; economy, 4, 55, 75, 80; ecosystem, 4; exchange, 8; gaps, xvi, 8, 22, 46, 107; work, 22, 80, 116, 117

Labor, 101; in academia, 69, 71, 72; contrasted with hustle, 16; devaluing, 12, 42, 71, 73; for graduate students, 72; joy in, 7; market, 18; unpaid, 9; value of, 4, 11, 35, 49, 69, 72, 79
Latino entrepreneurship, 5
Launching: business, 38, 44, 47, 55, 122, 140, 144, 153; Hikma, xvi, 2, 6, 9, 39, 146; newsletter, 20; plan, 24, 35, 38, 122, 131; resources, 151; website, 20
Law, practice of, 144
Learning, 75, 119, 129, 134, 136, 139; about clients, 69, 100, 102–3, 106; from clients, 131, 132, 133, 134, 150; capacity for, 39–40, 54, 108, 118; communities, 56, 110, 130; entrepreneurial, xvii, 2, 9, 11, 17, 22, 24, 27, 46, 54, 57, 59, 74, 78, 91, 94, 109, 110, 145; from feedback, 109; humanist enjoyment of, 7, 26, 39, 122; opportunities for, 11, 17, 26, 28, 42, 45, 53, 68, 110, 154; sharing, 5; skills, 81
LinkedIn, 140, 149
Literary Translators' Association of Canada, 85
Loans, 74, 145, 151–52; student, 77
Logo, business, 129
Logos, 47–49, *48*, *123*, *124*
London, England, xiv
Lorde, Audre, x, xi

"Making it," definition of, x
Malloy, Jonathan, 7, 27, 30, 53
Marketing, 5, 25, 38, 94, 129, 148–49; campaign, 24, 115; expenses, 75; strategy, 22, 25, 31, 47, 55, 128, 129, 131

Market research, 40, 42, 46, 86, 89, 91, 102, 131, 145, 152. *See also* Competitors
Master of Business Administration (MBA), 44
McKinsey & Company, 5
Medieval English literature, xiii, 29; Arabic influences on, 52
Medieval studies, xiii, xiv, 6, 52, 70, 144
Meetings, 51–52, 89, 90, 117; with business experts, 139; with potential clients, 101; pricing for, 59, 84; scope creep and, 63, 89. *See also* Clients, meetings with; Consultations
Menstrual products, 18
Mentoring, 22, 33, 46, 69, 76, 137–38, 150, 153; academic, 7, 72; network, 35; in teaching, 51
Meta, 31. *See also* Social media, X (formerly Twitter)
Middlebury Language Schools, xiii
Milwaukee, xiv, 15
Minimum viable product, 44, 56–58, 59, 129. *See also* Offers, core
Mizuta, Ai, 45
Mohammed, Rafi, 62
Money, ix, 2, 16, 24, 31, 90, 106, 114, 118, 119, 146, 147; amount necessary, 73, 74–75, 76, 77; asking for more, 117; and employees, 153; as evil, xi, 11–13, 150; and grants, 151; humanist attitudes about, 6, 11–13, 26, 69, 145, 150; and hypercapitalism, 17, 145; investors and, 152; profit, 74, 147–48; revenue, 75, 81; and scope creep, 113, 114; and social media, 148; time and, 69, 73, 106, 145; as a tool, x–xi, 12, 13, 69, 77, 150. *See also* Accounting; Investors; Profit; Revenue
Moten, Crystal Marie, 12, 15
Motivation, 26, 33, 79, 117, 119, 149
Mullaney, Thomas S., 10
Musk, Elon, 16, 33, 145
MyHours, 79, 146, 148

Naming your business, 129
National Endowment for the Humanities, xiv, xvi, 9
National Humanities Conference, x, 3
National Museum of African American History and Culture, 3
National Public Radio, 15

**170**  Index

Negotiation, 69, 71, 95, 103, 144, 160n1; with leadership, 4; pricing, 22, 40, 42, 68, 69, 71, 85, 86, 89; on projects, 9, 69, 71; scope of work and, 63

Neill, Bill, 97

Neoliberalism, 6, 15, 16

Neoplatonism, 98. *See also* Plato

Networking, 26, 27, 81, 138

Networks, 5, 23, 25, 43, 89, 90, 97, 131, 132, 152; mentoring, 35; social, 5, 95

Newsletter, 20, 72, 97–98, 129, 147, 151

Nonprofit organizations, xiv, 5, 23, 39, 90, 92

Offers, 35, 38, 56, 62, 68, 71, 75, 91, 132, 145; core, 38, 57–58, 59, 60–61, 65 (*see also* Minimum viable product); differentiating, 130; for extras, 117; pitching, 68

Office space, 31, 134, 144

Online presence, 128–29

Operations, business, 24–25, 69, 75, 78, 80, 140, 147–48; common expenses of, 138

Osterwalder, Alex, 57

Oxford University, xiii, 56

Pathos, 47–49, *48*, *123*, *124*

Payment, 2, 20, 42, 57, 78, 89, 103, 112, 146; checklist for, 137; collecting, 25; delays, 94; invoices and, 78, 94, 137, 146, 147; tracking, 146

Payroll, 75, *138*

Persuasion, Aristotelian principles of, 47–49, 68

Pitching, 68, 107

Plato, 13, 19. *See also* Neoplatonism

Podcasts, 41, 49, 55–56, 58, 59, 64, 72–73

Polarization, 2

Polis (start-up), 10

Postdocs, 24, 27, 41, 114

Poverty, ix. *See also* Financial precarity

Pricing, 18, 24, 38, 57, 59, 60, 71, *83*, 96, 97, 108, 145; baseline rate, 69, 78, 80, 82, 146; choosing a strategy, 2, 75, 78, 125; as communication, 35, 94; discounting, 63, 72, 118; hourly, 78–80, 82–85; market research and, 125, 127, *127*, 130; methods for establishing, 69, 91–92; models, 35, 65, 82–89; negotiating (*see* Negotiation, pricing); other models,

91; quotes, 80, 102, 103, 104, 110, 115, 117, 136, 137; raising, 102; revenue goals, calibrating to, 76; tiered (*see* Scope of work, tiered); undercharging, 12–13, 42, 71, 73, 92; by unit, 82, 85–86, 90, 125; value-based (*see* Value-based pricing); when to discuss, 103; working hours, 81. *See also* Contracts; Project rates; Value-based pricing

Princeton GradFUTURES Forum, 20, 27

Priorities, 73–74, 91–92, 99, 145, 146; clients', 61, 87, 103, 133; determining, xiv, xvi, 17, 27, 28, 56, 96; reflecting on, 30

Productizing. *See* Project rates

Product-market fit, 40

Professional development, 25, 39, 72–73, 75–76, 154; courses, 72

Profit, 12, 76, 80–81, 146, 147–48; definition of, 74; formula, 73–76, 81, 138, 140; tracking, 147–48. *See also* Money

Program evaluation, 55

Project management, 4, 52, 94, 112–13

Project rates, 62, 86, 88–89, 90, 114, 117, 125. *See also* Pricing; Value-based pricing

Prometheus, 13–14, 19

Proposals, 32, 81; book, 30; business, 35; client, 50, 58, 61, 63, 68, 71, 82, 87, 90, 92, 103, 107, 108, 149; grant (*see* Grant writing)

*Protagoras*, 13

Pryal, Katie Rose Guest, 72, 84

Publishing, scholarly, xiv, 86, 104

Racism, 15

Rea, Christopher, 10

Reagan era, 15

Reese, Barry (Cassidy), 15

Referrals, 20, 26, 42, 61, 94, 97, 99, 101, 110, 117, 140; meaningful, 96

Reflection, x, 17, 33, 58, 110, 122, 140, 146; in academia, 39; ahead, 62; on graduate school experience, 53–54; on pricing, 62, 88; on priorities, 27, 30; on process, 53–54; on strengths, 23; on value proposition, 123

Registering your business, 25, 81, 137, 145

Relationships, 4, 14, 16, 56; building, 8, 25, 40, 43, 49, 78, 97, 131; business as a product of, 20; client (*see* Clients, relationships with); with colleagues, xvi; communication in,

100, 101; expectations in, 103; feedback in, 149; free consult as a litmus test for, 102; professional, 8, 9, 28, 49, 56, 100, 110, 134; scope creep impact on, 112–13, 114

Rent the Runway, 57

Research, 7, 29, 30, 47, 52, 81, 134, 151, 153, 154; academic, 7, 8; definition of, 10; expertise in, 43, 47, 118; legal, 144; market (*see* Market research); as preparation for meetings with professionals, 139

Resilience, 8, 15, 17, 42, 46, 47, 122

Resources, 139; accountants, 24, 74, 75, 137, 139; banks, 24, 139, 151; financial advisers, 69, 137, 139; lawyers, 24, 74, 75, 137, 139; small business support organizations, 24, 137, 138, 139, 151

Résumés, 50–51, 52, 135

Retainers, 91

Retirement, 77

Revenue, 12, 74–76, 79, 80–81, 118, 138, 147, 151, 152, 153; definition of, 75; goals, 76, 80, 95, 119; Hikma's, 110; increasing, 94, 117; predicting, 42, 43, 90; tracking, 146, 147. *See also* Money

RevHub, 152

Rigor, 4, 8, 18, 19, 42

Risk, 14, 32; entrepreneurial, 15, 20, 46, 73, 77, 84, 110, 145; of scope creep, 112–13 (*see also* Scope creep)

Rituals, 33, 34

Rockefeller, John, 19

Rogers, Katina, 9

Rosario, Isabella, 15

Routine, daily, 31, 33

Salesforce, 148

Scholarship: community, 8–9; independent, 8

Scope creep, 41, 61, 63, 79, 112–13, 114, 116; reframing, 116–17. *See also* Contracts; Scope of work

Scope of work, 44, 65, 86, 92, 104, 108, 112–13, 125; boundaries and, 80; components of, 61; defining, 58–60; details to include, 59, 102; hourly rates and, 84; tiered, 38, 61–63, 88, 91, 125, *126*; value-based pricing and, 87–88, 89, 91. *See also* Contracts; Scope creep

Self-generation, 151

Services, *64*, 68–69, 101–2, 125, *127*; additional, 61, 108, 112, 113, 115, 116, 125 (*see also* Clients, extras for); agreement, 137; categories of, 146; clients, tailoring to, 95–96, 118; core, 124, 125; creation of, 46; department (in academia), 72; description of, 125; expanding, 55, 61–63, 90, 102, 116–17; feedback as, 110; identifying, 35, 43, 101, 130; "just in time," 40; parameters of, 59, 61, 92, 125; pricing (*see* Pricing); scoping (*see* Scope of work; Scope creep); simplifying, 55, 56–58; translating skills into, 22, 52, 53, 54; value of, 38, 49, 68, 94, 127; value propositions and (*see* Value propositions); volunteer, 72. *See also* Minimum viable product; Proposals; Scope creep

Shaw, Madeleine, 12, 16, 17–18

Side gigs. *See* Side hustle

Side hustle, xvi, 4, 5, 9, 24, 38, 43, 70, 75, 89; accidental, 40, 41, 42; priorities of, 73

Skepticism, 6, 11, 16, 44

Skills, 11, 17, 27, 39, 45, 49, 57, 98, 110, 118, 153; analysis, 47; communication, 97; compensation commensurate with, 71–72; dissertation, 52–53; learning new, 81, 90, 97, 118; making a difference with, x, xi; marketable, 9; research, 47, 154; soft, 4; teaching, 50–52, *51*; translating, 22, 38, 43–44, 50, 55; translation of languages, 70; value of, 29, 40, 42, 43–44. *See also* Career competencies

Small Business Administration, 138, 139

Small Business BC, 138, 139

Smithsonian Institution, xiv, 3

Social enterprise, 17, 19, 22

Social media, 8, 14, 20, 31, 47, 55, 64, 128, 148; auditing, 128; campaign, 25; handles, 128. *See also* Meta; Online presence; X (formerly Twitter)

Solomon, Joel, 12

Spence, Lester K., 16

Start-up companies, 2, 4, 10, 11, 14, 18, 40, 47, 145, 147; bros, 14, 33; culture, 17; early-stage, 56; founders, 13, 40; funding, 152; humanist attitudes about, 44; hypercapitalism in, 17–18; incubators, 22, 152, 162n4; vocabulary, 44, 47, 61, 103, 151

Storytelling, 25, 55–56, 119, 128, 129, 130, 131, 153; entrepreneurship as, 45; humanist skills in,

172 Index

Storytelling (*continued*)
4, 13, 127; in launch, 35; leveraging, 22; in pricing, 68, 87, 91

Strengths, x, 17, 20, 23, 68, 110, 144, 154; curiosity as, 40; of the humanities, 3, 10–11; in launching a business, 153; leveraging, 38, 53; and marketing strategies, 25; in others, 3, 4, 22; recognizing, 22, 44, 62, 122, 153; translating, 35, 38

Stress, 31, 47, 88, 106, 113. *See also* Anxiety

St. Scholastica Day Riots, xiii, 56

Students, xiii, xiv, 43, 51, 52, 108, 113; graduate, xvi, 2, 24, 27, 38, 39, 40, 50, 53, 71, 72, 98

Sustainability, xi, xvi, 3, 12, 13–14, 18, 19

Target market, 46, 130

Taxes, 2, 18, 25, 74, 137, 139, 144, 146, 147

Teaching, ix–x, 4, 49, 56, 108; in academia, xiv, 30, 41, 104; advantages of, 51–52; as an entrepreneur, xvi, 31; facilitation, compared to, 52; online, 52; self-teaching, 10–11; translatable skills of, 4, 40, 50–52, 51

Tenure, 7

Tenure track, xiv, 6, 29–30, 47; job market, xvi, 2, 98

Testimonials, 70, 90, 129, 149

*Tiger King*, 31

Time, 82–83; with family, xiv; as a finite resource, 56, 61, 73; nonbillable, 73, 78, 81, 84; prioritizing, 17, 73; recording (*see* Hours worked, tracking and reporting); saving, 17, 25; tensions around, 106; value of, 71, 84, 101, 102; values and, 30

Toggl, 79, 146, 148

Town/gown relations, xiii, 56

Translation, 55, 58, 59, 70, 86–87, 89–90, 114–15; entrepreneurship, compared to, 3, 10–11; as a hustle, 10, 38, 55, 58, 70, 82, 114–15; medieval, xiii; pricing, 59, 85, 86–87, 89–90, 95, 114–15; of skills, 22, 35, 38, 44, 48, 50, 53, 68

Tutoring, 38, 55, 58, 59, 82

Twitter. *See* X (formerly Twitter)

Tworek, Michael, 10

Uncertainty, 47, 73, 106; of entrepreneurship, 32, 46, 74, 122; of project rates, 88. *See also* Ambiguity

Underemployment, 8, 9

United Nations Sustainable Development Goals, 3, 13, 19

University of British Columbia, 7, 17, 27, 138, 152; Arts Amplifier, 27

University of California–Irvine Humanities Center, 27

University of Notre Dame, xiii, 47

Value-based pricing, 62, 86–89, 90, 91, 125. *See also* Pricing; Project rates

Value proposition, 38, 44, 47–50, *48*, 65, 68, 123–24, *123*, 128, 130, 131

Vancouver, Canada, xiv, 33

van Hees, Sophia, 33

Van Wyck, James, 17

Venture capital, 5, 152, 162n4; equity gaps in, 5. *See also* Investors

Washington, DC, xiv

Waste management, 14

Webb, Andrea, 7, 39

Website, 55, *64*, 75, 90, 114–15, *127*; analytics, 147, 148; auditing, 128; content of, 70, 130; expenses, 138; launching, 20, 129; market research on, 130–31

Weisbuch, Robert, 10

Williams, Mary Evelyn, 15

Wins, celebrating, 20, 33, 140, 149

Wisconsin Supreme Court, 144

Women, x, 15; Black women, ix, x, 15; of color, ix, x, 15, 73; entrepreneurship, attitudes about, 16; in the humanities, 16; rights, 18; and venture capital funding, 5

Workaholism, 14

Workshops, 20, 27

Writing accountability group, 97

X (formerly Twitter), 31, 52

Y Combinator, 152

Zeus, 14

Zoom, xvi, 31

Zuckerberg, Mark, 145

# About the Authors and Illustrator

**Erica Machulak**, PhD, is the founder and lead facilitator of Hikma, a social impact start-up with a mission to mobilize scholarship for the public good through consulting, training, and storytelling. Since completing her dissertation on Arabic influences in medieval English literature, she has written articles for *Inside Higher Ed*, *Intellect Ltd*, and *Humanities*, the magazine of the National Endowment for the Humanities. She holds degrees from the University of Pennsylvania (BA), the University of Oxford (MSt), and the University of Notre Dame (PhD).

**Crystal Marie Moten**, PhD, is a public historian, curator, and writer who focuses on the intersection of race, class, and gender to uncover the hidden histories of Black people in the Midwest. She holds degrees from Washington University in Saint Louise (BA) and the University of Wisconsin, Madison (MA/PhD). She is the author of the award-winning book *Continually Working: Black Women, Community Intellectualism and Economic Justice in Postwar Milwaukee*.

**Sophia van Hees**, PhD, is a multipassionate creative with a background ranging from fine art to cognitive neuroscience. She takes an experimental approach to her business and design work, weaving together threads of ideas to discover new and unpredictable connections along the way. As the owner of Brave Snail Designs, she also embraces fearless creativity mixed with slow and meaningful growth. She holds a bachelor of speech pathology and a PhD from the University of Queensland, Australia.